VOLUME 2

STAND UP!

Resilient Black Women Who Are Shaping the World With Their *Faith*

VISIONARY AUTHOR
ArDenay Garner

©Copyright 2022 ArDenay Garner

All rights reserved. This book is protected under the copyright laws of the United States of America.

ISBN-13: 978-1-954609-36-5

Library of Congress Control Number: 2021925066

No portion of this book may be reproduced, distributed, or transmitted in any form, including photocopying, recording, or other electronic or mechanical methods, without the written permission of the publisher, except in the case of brief quotations embodied in reviews and certain other non-commercial uses permitted by copyright law. Permission granted on request.

For information regarding special discounts for bulk purchases, please contact the publisher:
LaBoo Publishing Enterprise, LLC
staff@laboopublishing.com
www.laboopublishing.com

The Holy Bible, King James Version. Cambridge Edition: 1769; *King James Bible Online*, 2019. www.kingjamesbibleonline.org.

Scripture taken from the New King James Version®. Copyright © 1982 by Thomas Nelson. Used by permission. All rights reserved.

Scripture quotations marked TPT are from The Passion Translation®. Copyright © 2017, 2018 by Passion & Fire Ministries, Inc. Used by permission. All rights reserved. ThePassionTranslation.com.

CONTENTS

Introduction 1

little girl in a Grown Women's skin©
~ Dr. Carlene M. Lacey. 5

Peace in the Storm ~ Natalie Reeves 17

A Beautiful Broken Masterpiece ~ Cecilia White 29

After the Storm – I Am Her ~ Antoinette D. Washington 41

Healed As They Went ~ Tymesha Sene. 55

Your Purpose Will Find You ~ Robin Young 65

From Shattered Shards, Solace ~ Samantha JC Pierce 75

Mom Said, "Rise and Be Counted!" ~ Denika Lundy. 85

Lessons From Lou ~ Yolanda C. Brown 97

Anger ~ Melinda Agnew. 109

Chaos Breaking Faith ~ Sherry S. Beam. 125

Connecting the Dots His Way, Not Mine
~ Deborah Maddox. 135

Unfinished ~ Rev. Ardella Angela Young 149

About the Visionary Author 161

"Healing doesn't mean the damage never existed; it means the damage no longer controls our lives."

Akshay Dubey

INTRODUCTION

God has called thirteen Resilient Black Women Authors from behind the curtain to STAND UP, unmute their voices, write their personal stories of tribulation and victory, and help others heal. This collection of personal stories will help you rediscover the truth of who you really are underneath the proverbial mask of shame, doubt, and fear. *STAND UP! Resilient Black Women Who Are Shaping The World With Their Faith Volume 2* will inspire you to find meaning in your painful experiences from the past so that you can forgive yourself for believing that you were broken, unworthy, not lovable, not important, not good enough, too old, or forsaken by God.

Often, when you are going through troubling times, you may feel alone. You convince yourself that no one understands your situation. You believe that you are the "only one" to experience this type of heartache and pain and you run, hide, and withdraw from your family and friends, only to feel more isolated, depressed, and discouraged. These stories serve as a reminder that you are never alone. There are women who identify with your pain and have overcome and are still overcoming by the grace of God. The authors wrote their personal stories to inspire your healing journey.

Resilient Black Women Authors are courageous women dedicated to promoting compassion and world healing through storytelling. Our mission is to uproot and address generational trauma in the Black community that has been silenced and ignored. We are breaking our silence and speaking our truth about experiences that catapulted our personal growth and spiritual development—experiences that forced us to seek a deeper, more intimate relationship with God. Whether it was abuse or rejection from a parent, sudden death of a loved one, abandonment by a mate, incarceration of a child, illness, or loss of identity and sense of self, we are expressing our truth. In the process, we have healed at a deeper level, released the shame and guilt that has held us hostage, and provided a prescription for you to do the same.

There was a period in life when I desperately wanted external validation. I tried to be perfect so others could not detect the depth of my insecurities, my negative self-concept, my fear of rejection, my desperate desire to be in a loving relationship, or my fear of failing my children and God. I was hiding in plain sight. Whenever I stepped outside my home, I would be in full costume— a two-piece Tahari suit or Calvin Klein dress, single strand of pearls, high heels, custom wig, manicured nails, MAC lip gloss, drenched in Christian Dior fragrance. I presented as the poster child of having it "all together" because I believed that was required for Black women in corporate America. We had to work twice as hard and be on our "A" game at all times. We are expected to be strong and maintain an unrealistic balance between work, family, and extracurricular activities. Somewhere along the way we convinced ourselves that asking for help was a sign of weakness or laziness, and so we did not ask for help or support. Black women had to be strong at all costs, even if it cost us our sanity.

Black people were taught early in life to "keep folks out of our business" and not to talk about family matters outside of the household. We were sworn to a life of secrecy and we learned to suppress our emotions. While that approach may have worked for our parents and grandparents, as a forty-five-year-old woman

Introduction

experiencing the aftermath of the COVID-19 pandemic, I know it is not an effective approach for the 21st century. We can no longer afford to suffer in silence. Our mental health is at stake. Our young people need to know how we survived adversity. They need to know what made us resilient when all odds were against us. They need examples of how we demonstrated faith in moments of fear and uncertainty. This is the Resilient Black Women Authors' antidote to eradicating generational trauma through storytelling. When we share our stories of resilience, faith, perseverance, survivorship, reconciliation, and forgiveness we empower others to reflect on their own experiences to find meaning in the messiness of life. A common theme you will notice is each author's journey of finding herself in the midst of chaos, trauma, abuse, and illness. Pain is a great teacher. It forces us to examine our situation and decide how we want to respond. We can choose to do nothing and remain in pain, we can choose to do what we have always done and get the same outcome, or we can choose to do something different to reduce or eliminate the pain. Healing is a personal choice. Each author chose to do something *different* to shape the world with their faith and start the inward healing process.

It is my prayer that *STAND UP! Resilient Black Women Who Are Shaping The World With Their Faith Volume 2* will inspire you to give yourself permission to address your emotional wounds and make healing your personal responsibility.

inJOY,

ArDenay

Dr. Carlene Lacey's creative entrepreneurial spirit is evidenced as an author, a career coach, inspirational speaker and real estate professional. Carlene takes a vision and makes it reality through sound strategy development. She intuitively sees the threads of opportunity within an organization and brings them together into a coherent whole.

She is an inspirational leader who inspires action while remaining grounded in financial information that levers the business. Respected as a credible voice in decision making, finding strategic partners, and establishing governance boundaries, Carlene earns a seat at the table wherever she serves.

Dr. Carlene Lacey is an avid learner and has earned her Doctoral degree in Management and Organizational Leadership, Masters Business Administration and Bachelor's in Human Resource Management. She lives in Upstate New York with her family.

little girl in a Grown Women's skin©

Dr. Carlene M. Lacey

little girl in a Grown Women's skin©

I'm just a little girl in a grown women's skin;
arrested development lurks within.

I'm just a little girl trapped in a women's skin;
Unresolved feelings of abandonment trying to do me in.

The only remembrance is an ache,
longing for continuity…
unable to communicate.
The emptiness I felt when loved ones left…
not knowing the day or time of their return.
Left to cope with all the mess.

I'm not trying to remain angry…
the emotions just rage within.

STAND UP!

Hating those I Love…
Loving those I hate…
Has me trapped in a world of confusion.

As I go about day to day trying to express myself,
In an uninsulting way, still, I am left feeling…
UNHEARD, UNDERMINNED, and UNCARED FOR.

Time heals all wounds, they say…
but I know my battle within is because the wounds
that are masked by perfection constantly stab me,
like a knife poking through plastic…

Eventually, the hole appears, allowing fluids of
injustice, jealousy, envy, and strife to seep in.

How can I change these feelings that are so very real?

You say GROW UP!

I ask HOW!

When I'm just a little girl trapped in a grown women's skin.

Mama, don't leave me –
you are not aware what happens when you're gone –
heck, you've been emotionally absent since the day that I was born!

Daddy, don't leave me; 'cause when you do, sorrow overshadows my day,
like on the day you left and I longed for your return – and I have to dull
that feeling even to this day!

Brother, don't ignore me, because I long to hear your voice.
It saddens me to
think that not speaking to me is your choice.

And if life had not dealt me enough blows before the age of ten,
the worst came when my title was stripped –
no longer the Baby, again!
How did I have my title stripped by mommy and daddy too?
Both found other lovers and produced a child, without asking my opinion.

Yet I was forced to love this helpless soul that needed me to care for it.
Teaching, watching, training, and loving were tasks I did not sign up for.

Did anyone care what I thought –
moving from state to state, across the land…
No! and that is why,
I'm trapped in a grown women's skin!

It angers me to no end to see children captivate their parent's attention…
could it be jealousy,
could it be envy,
or could it just be that those skills remain untrained.

Don't judge me until you have walked in my shoes.
insecure in my own skin, in a world that constantly changes…
seeing beneath the words, reading between the lines; understanding the nuances;
has been a curse of mine.

Don't feel sorry for me either…
about my struggle that lies within; the one thing
that has been constant is God has cultivated the…

little girl that plays freely, in a grown Women's skin!

    I still remember the day when the words of this poem came pouring out of my spirit as I released a tsunami of tears. Writing feverishly to express my feelings of frustration, uncertainty and tethering on the verge of despair, again! "Little girl in a grown woman's skin" turned out to be one of my most intense writings—my masterpiece. Finally, I had given myself permission to proclaim my secret place openly. I felt naked and relieved at the same time. Acknowledging my roots ignited my passion to understand my resilient journey through love, transition and validation.

Love

I grew up searching for love and trying to understand the depth of the word that was at times spoken by others often, sparingly by others, and at times never spoken.
    The love of a mother, the love of a father, the love of a child, the love of a spouse, the love of a sibling, the love of a friend.
    There are stages of love: conception, action and aftermath.
    Love, adoration, yearning to speak with, to be with, to please, to protect and ultimately to release. Love is to honor, respect, and yes, submit and obey are also characteristics of love. Scripture tells us that Love covers a multitude of sins. Love chastens and, contrary to your belief, it sometimes separates.
    If you have ever experienced Love, it transcends beyond the feeling of butterflies in your stomach when your significant other

is in your presence. It transcends the lust when engaged in the physical act of pleasure that has the ability to procreate an example of that moment. Love: the moment when you first feel the flutter of life within your womb or hear from a distant friend.

Love is often described as an intense emotion that can at times blind one's senses. Love....

Its infamous beauty cannot compare to the Love that is in God, the Love that awaits us who tap into the source, the Father, the King and his name is Jehovah. Master, Teacher, Healer.

It is in those moments that when you are STILL that you can take in the breath of the moment. Your soul can experience the fullness of Joy that exists in HIM.

Be still and know that I am God!

I hear the Lord saying...

Drop those things that you hold in your hand and place your hand in the Master's Hand.

Turn your attention from those things that you hold precious and watch God fill them with His glory.

Loosen your affections from all others, and place in His hands those whom you hold dear. Leave them in the keeping of God.

When you do this your heart can be set free to seek the Lord your God without distraction.

For when I AM becomes more precious than everything and everyone else;

When I AM becomes more real than all else;

When we love I AM more than we love any other, only then can we know complete satisfaction.

Only then can we understand the meaning in "the Joy of the Lord is my Strength" (Nehemiah 8:10).

Embracing Christ Jesus as my Lord provided me the courage to peek into my past, while providing me the opportunity to experience joy – a state of contentment in spite of the circumstances. On my resilient journey, I learned my love is always near and the joy of my Lord is my confidence in tremulous times and my balancer in times of exuberance.

Validation

Everyone yearns to receive validation.

Why am I here; why does this or that matter?

As soon as I began to learn that much of the help I provided to others was to receive validation from others, I got still. I began to listen to the voice inside of me, the whisper that kept saying, "Carlene, what do you want? How do you want to live your life? Does this align with how you see yourself? Your vision being played out?"

When I began to answer those questions, it was scary. I always, even as a young girl, thought about others or had to adjust based on the actions of others. I had to go along to get along. But it became real apparent that my actions were benefiting others to my own detriment.

Something had to change. Today, I do believe that relationships are fundamental to a fulfilled life; however, not at the cost of my wellbeing. I have chosen to be intentional in my decisions, accepting their unintentional consequences.

I am learning that my life is big and my light shines bright, and sometimes my brightness scares others because they are not ready to receive me. I am learning to be a spotlight and have my rays be adjustable to shine on areas, people and things that will illuminate the essence of me, illuminate the I Am in me, permeating the darkness in which I embark, whether the unconscious thoughts of negativity that fill my dome or the flagrant mishandling of others that I wade through like the condensed mud in a swamp. My intentionality allows me the freedom to choose life, in spite of what comes my way.

Let me be clear: Like you, I yearn to hear "well done," "you matter" or "I love you." However, today it is less about my hearing those words and receiving validation from others and more about receiving continued validation from Christ.

My conversation with Christ about my family and friends is "forgive them, Father, for they know not what they do, and grant me the courage to forgive them as you have forgiven me."

Transition

It is amazing that when it is time for God to transition you, it often comes at a time when you may not feel adequately prepared. God's word declares that he takes the foolish things to confound the wise. There are instances in our lives when it just does not make sense, when we have to prepare to move out of the way for the next phase.

What I have learned throughout the years is that it is an uncomfortable awkwardness that cannot be articulated. You have followed the commands of the Father; when he said move, you did just that. When he said stand still, you followed that command with obedience. When he said follow those who have authority (as they follow me); again, you proceeded. Each act of obedience led to increased confidence and trust in hearing the voice of the Lord. Soon, your steps ordered by the Lord were swift and the gallop like a horse turned into the stride of a gazelle! Being in tune with the Lord allows you to dance with a rhythm that flows in sync with the Heavenlies. The Divine is expressing itself through your life in a way that is evident without your audible testimony.

It is in those times that all hell can be breaking loose, or even worse, the Lord says, "It is time to move!" What? Did I hear correctly? Yes, it is time to move. Move from the comfort of your current circumstances. Move from the quiet reliance on your position in the ranks. Move to dependence on the Lord your God.

Immediately, fear raises its ugly head. Who do you think you are? You are not qualified. Nobody has done that before. You are not as good as... you fill in the blank. Why don't you stay where you are? You are in a good place. You should stay where you are because you are going to get the same thing in the next experience. You all have heard one or more of these statements. If you have not, you may be the one speaking them to others.

There are a few instances that come to mind that taught me valuable lessons:

The first lesson I learned is that people are more apt to help you as long as you are in need and don't pose a threat to their livelihood.

When I was earning my undergraduate degree, my manager told me that as long as my work was done, I could work on my schoolwork. This was a fantastic benefit for my employer to provide and I took advantage and completed my Bachelor of Science degree. However, an unexpected awkwardness was present when I pursued my Master's in Business Administration; that same benefit of finishing my school assignments when my work was done became strained...

It was confusing at first; however, it was later revealed that I was embarking on the same degree as my manager and it was uncomfortable for her as I got closer to the completion because transition was evident.

Another valuable lesson learned along my journey is that people who receive a word to move often delay because of an enduring relationship.

I was on my educational journey with my father, and throughout the experience my father was extremely wise; he was diligent in his study, choosing a topic that was of interest to him. He was in senior management and commanded the respect of his peers, even more because he was pursuing the upper echelon of his education. Meanwhile, I had just entered middle management when starting the same education program. I chose a study that was meaningful and consistent with my destiny. We were doing it together and it was amazing. Often, there were calls talking about the research and the highs and lows of the process; it was fantastic being on the same journey with my father.

My father moved consistently through his program but unexpectedly experienced a lull, a block, during his dissertation process. Meanwhile, I moved through my educational journey and obstacles with precision – inclusive of almost being expelled for a technicality. There came a time when I was at a point of submitting the first draft of the dissertation and fear rose. How can I submit this? Following my father has brought me this far and passing him now will take me into uncharted waters. Doubt and insecurity set in like rigor mortis.

So I delayed. But only for a moment—the first draft was submitted to the mentor, the refinements completed. The second draft was submitted to the mentor, the refinements completed. The swiftness of the refinements of the first draft caused me to reach the doorway of transition. It was time to submit the dissertation to the committee. Doubt, fear, and feelings of inadequacy shouted loudly in my head. I became anxious and after two to three days of waiting, began to rush God for an answer. NOT APPROVED was the subject line.

Lesson learned – before submitting the corrected dissertation, the next time, prayer and supplication were submitted beforehand, and diligence in the art of patience was exercised. Every time doubt tried to arise, I pulled out the scripture in Philippians 4:6-7: 'Be anxious for nothing but in all things, through prayer and supplication with thanksgiving make your request known unto God and the peace of God which surpasses all understanding shall keep your heart and mind in Christ Jesus.' Keeping our mind focused on Christ Jesus is the secret sauce.

After I submitted the corrected dissertation, I relinquished control and waited patiently, giving God continuous praise for two weeks. I did not make the mistake of doubting; each moment I spoke life by putting the word of God on my situation. In expectation of a positive report, I looked for the final decision. While waiting, I received a letter from one of my credit lenders which read 'Congratulations' – and that was the fuel I needed to continue trusting and affirming the completion. Well, as you might imagine, notification of the decision came: Congratulations, your dissertation is APPROVED. Your body of work has now been added as a doctoral scholar in human resource management, organizational leadership and succession planning. I dropped to the floor, right in my office. The taste of completion is only second to salvation!

As I reflect on my achievement, joy fills my heart. I am reminded that the end of a thing marked the beginning of a new journey. The true essence of love lives on through the triumphant victory of purpose fulfilled. A testament that God will choose the foolish things to confound the wise is that my resilient journey to complete my doctoral degree began with the painful yet beautiful transition of my baby.

Resilience

The one thing that is constant is change. You are either coming out of something, going through something, or about to go into something. These are the stages of change. Your resilience is revealed when you press on and keep going through adversity, doubt, insecurity and pain. Resilience is what I call 'snap back'. It is the ability press toward the mark, the high calling which is in Christ Jesus.

Throughout my resilient journey there are moments that serve as the chisel to shape this pot of clay, moments that left me with a choice to either be bitter or better; moments that gave way for me to slip but not sink, to falter but not fall; moments that provided clarity to dismal situations and love in the midst of hatred.

Beloved, as you read this epistle, know that life will have its twists and turns but you will 'snap back'. Don't get me wrong; there are times when you will want to quit. If you can get out of your own way and run on a little farther to see what the end may bring, you win.

Love, transition and resilience are the tools God allows me to use to enjoy my journey. I no longer search for love because I am love. Armed with the knowledge that love exists in all of us, I now welcome the expressed love of others and all its complexities. Whether hurting, ashamed, silent or conversational, joyful or bitter – love conquers all. When love is at the core, we are able to endure and grow. Love provides meaning in transition. It gives us hope for a new chapter and strength that others see as resilience.

Our experiences are woven together into the tapestry of life. It is important to remember that all things work together for our good and God's glory. As I stated in the beginning, the struggles on my resilient journey have cultivated the little girl who plays freely in a Grown Women's skin.

Born in Syracuse, NY, and raised in Harlem, NY, **Natalie Reeves** is the mother of three living children, one deceased child and the grandmother of four. She is employed as a hall monitor with the Syracuse City School District.

A born-again believer in Jesus Christ, her favorite scripture is John 3:16, "For God so loved the world, that he gave his only begotten Son, that whosoever believeth in him should not perish, but have everlasting life."

On December 18, 2011, Natalie accepted her calling to proclaim the good news of salvation through Jesus Christ. She is the Founder, CEO, and host of Sharing Faith Through Testimony, a vision given by God and birthed during the COVID-19 pandemic in 2020. Sharing Faith Through Testimony is a ministry that provides a platform for believers to share their personal testimony bringing glory to God and helping others to experience hope, joy and changed hearts. Watch Sharing Faith Through Testimony every third Sunday of the month at four o'clock eastern standard time on Facebook and YouTube.

PEACE IN THE STORM

Trials come to test and strengthen our faith at the same time. Eighteen years ago, my faith was truly tested. God carried me through one of the most trying seasons of my life, and my faith in God held me together.

The following testimony is not a typical experience. Reflecting back, I am still amazed at how I made it through, but as I recount these details the way I remember them, I am more sure now that God gave me peace in the storm. Forgiveness, justice, rest, strength, surrender, covering, endurance, and resilience are things only God could provide during a season that should have taken away my joy.

A 20-year-old man died on Wednesday night, May 12, 2004, after being shot at East Fayette and Allen street, police said. Police did not identify the victim pending notification of relatives. Officers patrolling near the intersection heard several gunshots about 10:30 pm that night, police spokesman Sgt. Tom Connellan said. They found the man lying outside a house at the southwest corner of East Fayette and Allen, opposite Rolling Green Estates apartment complex. He suffered several gunshot wounds. The man was taken to University

Hospital, where he was pronounced dead about 11:05 pm. - The Post-Standard

That 20-year-old was my oldest son, Patrick H. Felder, born October 24, 1983, in Syracuse, New York, to Natalie R. Reeves and Patrick Felder. A life resident of Syracuse, NY, he played football and basketball at Nottingham High School, where he graduated from the Syracuse City School District. He attended Herkimer Community College, was a member of the Boys and Girls Club, was employed as a Customer Service Representative at the Sutherland Group, and also worked part-time at Sears Inc.

A believer in Jesus Christ, Patrick was a member of the Bellegrove Missionary Baptist Church, where he was baptized and played the drums. In his spare time, he enjoyed playing drums and listening to music, collecting basketball, football, and baseball cards, and spending time with his family and friends. Patrick was a devoted son, brother, nephew, uncle, grandson, great-grandson and friend to all who knew him.

A night I'll never forget

It was a Wednesday night. I came home from Bible study and got Patrick's younger brothers ready for bed, as there was school the next day. After finally getting the boys settled down and into bed, I attempted to get a good night's sleep after a long day. With my body not ready to sleep, I decided to curl up in my bed and read my Bible until I felt myself getting tired. It wasn't long before the phone rang. As I answered the phone, all I heard was commotion in the background and a young lady screaming, "Lumpy's been shot!" I immediately knew "Lumpy" was Patrick, as he had been given this nickname because he was born with a lump on his head. I heard it again: "Lumpy's been shot."

Denial

I paused, knowing what I heard and refusing to believe it, instead thinking she was not calm enough to clearly tell me why she called. I asked her to try and calmly repeat herself.

She said, "Lumpy's been shot." I asked her where she was and she said, "Fayette and Allen." I dropped my phone and dropped to my knees, asking God to help me.

Bargaining

I lay on the floor, in shock and unable to move. I had no idea whether my son would be dead or alive once I made it to the scene. I said, "This can't be true, Lord," but I knew there was no way I could make it without talking to the Lord first. This is where my testimony takes a different turn. I immediately went into prayer, saying, "I've experienced great trouble before but nothing of this magnitude ever. I don't know how much more I can take, but God help me. Please don't let this be true."

Depression

Before I could even stand, a still, small voice reminded me of the words spoken by Jesus Christ while in the Garden of Gethsemane. In agony He said to the Father, "If it be possible, let this cup pass from me" (Matthew 26:39). These are the exact words I remember crying out to Jesus while on my knees with tears running down my face, asking God to save my son. "Lord, please don't let Patrick die. God, don't let my son die."

Acceptance

While still lying there on the floor and begging God, I was led by the Holy Spirit to shift my request, with my new prayer now being, "Lord, if this is my child, please don't let them take my son away until I get there." I found myself quoting Jesus Christ again as he spoke to his Father, saying, "Nevertheless not my will, but your will be done" (Luke 22:42).

It was at that very moment of distress that I felt the Lord's presence and God provided me with supernatural strength to get up off the floor. I had accepted that the Lord alone knows the scope of His deeds on earth and there remained nothing else for me to do but yield to his will. After getting up from the floor, the next events seemed like a blur. I checked on my youngest sons, who were still sleeping, left the house and drove myself to the crime scene. I arrived to a crowd of people, and all I heard was screaming and crying. I tried to drive closer but couldn't get through the crowd, so I jumped out of my car and walked the rest of the way.

I prayed that God would allow me to get to the ambulance before they left, and God honored my prayer. After fighting my way through the crowds, I got close enough to the body that was lying on the stretcher. I asked the paramedic if I could see the victim who had been shot, as I was told my son was the victim, and he pulled back the white sheet that was covering Patrick's face. When I looked at my baby, more tears flooded from my eyes. My heart was so heavy and full of hurt and pain. I walked away not really knowing if my son was dead or alive or where I was going, but just trying to get away from the chaos. That night had me so confused, I couldn't even remember where I parked my car. So many people were trying to console me as I was trying to leave. I didn't want to be bothered; I was focused on finding my car so I could follow the ambulance to the hospital in hopes that they could save my son's life.

I remember sitting in the waiting room with family and friends, waiting for the doctors to update us on Patrick's status. Sitting there, I felt the presence of the Lord comforting me and giving me peace in the midst of the storm. I heard that still, small voice again, this time saying, "Blessed are they that mourn: for they shall be comforted." That scripture came alive to me that very night and in that moment, God spoke and said, "I got him." That next moment, the physician on duty came out and informed me that Patrick didn't survive, but my heart was already prepared for this.

A Personal Miracle

The night I laid eyes on my son while he lay on the stretcher in the middle of the street, I was reminded of how hard it was for me when the paramedics pulled back the sheet so I could identify him. I will never forget what his countenance looked like, how his eyes and mouth were closed, with a sad expression on his face. Yet the day I had to identify Patrick's body at the morgue, God gave me my own personal miracle. God allowed me to see something different when the curtains were pulled back. My son's countenance had changed from his eyes and mouth being closed to them both being slightly opened with a slight smile on his face. It is hard for people to believe me when I retell this part of my story, but this personal miracle was for me to be able to give glory to God. God is the only one who can perform a miracle like this. He allowed me to witness with my own eyes the transfiguration of my son and allowed two others to witness what I saw while at the morgue. I knew it had to be nobody but God. In the street, my son had a sad countenance, yet the day after the doctors confirmed he had passed, I was able to see my son with a smile, indicating a joy only God could give to him.

The Prophecy

I now take you back to four days before the death of my son. My parents recall that it was the Saturday before Mother's Day. My father and mother are the pastor and first lady of a church. While they were closing out a prayer service, God spoke through my mother through the gift of prophecy. She stood up, and with her hand formed into the shape of a cup, began speaking to my father, saying, "This is a bitter cup. I don't know who this is for, but this is a bitter cup." At the time, my mother and father couldn't even imagine they would be hearing the gunshots that would kill their oldest grandson just four days later. Patrick loved his grandparents and oftentimes he would stop by their home to check on them and help them with anything they may have needed done. The day after God gave my mother the prophecy was Mother's Day. Patrick showed up at their house, not knowing that it would be the last time that his grandparents would ever see him alive.

On the night of May 12, 2004, when Patrick was shot, my dad recalls hearing shots being fired. While the shooting took place five blocks away, my father describes the sounds of the gunshots as though they occurred directly in front of their home. They did not know it was their grandson until their daughter called. To this day, I do not remember calling my parents. I do remember my mother telling me that my dad almost had a heart attack that night after hearing the news. My father recalls being unable to get out of the car and feeling like his heart was going to burst out of his chest. The prophecy came to pass and it was indeed a bitter cup.

Forgiveness

Nobody but God could give me the peace to release my feelings of resentment and forgive the person who murdered my son. Whether they actually deserved my forgiveness or not, I just knew in my heart there was no room for unforgiveness. The negative consequences of not forgiving others or yourself can lead to emotional hurt, anger, pain, hate, resentment, bitterness and more. I couldn't allow any of these things to take up residence in my heart because I knew that God would be the ultimate judge of sin. Because I forgave, my daily prayer for my son's murderer is that they have repented and asked God for forgiveness in the time since my son's death.

For those of you reading this, I can imagine what you are thinking. I understand that forgiving someone who has caused you pain and suffering is a difficult thing to do: "But God..." Jesus is our example of ultimate forgiveness. He forgave those who crucified him. He said, "Father, forgive them" (Luke 23:34). I am just thankful to God that during this tragic time in my life, He was with me in my darkest hour while I had to walk through the valley of the shadow of death (Psalm 23:4).

Looking Back

The five stages of grief are: denial, bargaining, anger, depression and acceptance. During this experience, I went through every stage except anger. I should have been angry—with God, with myself, with the shooter, with anyone. I had the right to be angry. God allowed me to experience my human emotions but spared me when it came to anger. Why anger? Because eighteen years later the killer has not been caught. I never allowed Patrick to play with water guns, toy guns or any toy weapons while he was growing up, but he ended up dying by gun violence. I have not heard anything from the District Attorney in 18 years. I used to call often, asking questions and every time I called, I would get the same answer, which was no answer. "Nothing yet, Ms. Reeves. We're still investigating the homicide and as soon as we hear something we'll contact you." At some point, I stopped calling and God reminded me, "Vengeance is mine, saith the lord" (Romans 12:19).

I did not want to retaliate. I simply desired justice. I began to question whether the police were even looking for my son's shooter because so many of our young Black men were still losing their lives to gun violence. There was gun violence everywhere, from the South side to the East side, the North side and West side. Over and over again the news spoke about drive-by shootings, oftentimes causing even innocent babies to lose their lives. This experience led me to become more involved in my community. I participated in Mothers against Gun Violence, founded by Helen Hudson, and took every opportunity presented to me to share my story. I felt it was my duty to support other mothers experiencing the same grief.

As I reflect over the events that occurred eighteen years ago, so many things about this specific testimony opened my eyes to the status of my relationship with God, and all I can do is thank Him that I made it through. As I write this, a number of things our happening simultaneously: I am sitting in the very house my parents sat in when they heard the gunshots. The date of my son's passing came and left. I read over the cards my youngest son's classmates gave him when his brother passed. I can still hear the voices of my parents as they recalled the incidents that occurred over the course of those few days. As I write this, two more tragic incidents of gun violence occurred just a week apart. Ten people were murdered in a grocery store just two hours from my home in Buffalo, NY. In Uvalde, Texas, nineteen young lives were taken, along with two teachers. Gun violence is out of control while city officials fail to regulate gun control.

Looking back, I must acknowledge the fact that I never would have made it through this difficult time without the support of my family and friends. God placed three strong women in my life who played a significant part in helping me during this time. I remember feeling God's protection, and He used these women to make sure I was comforted during the entire time before my son's funeral. I can honestly say they covered me from having to engage with a lot of people so that God could keep me still. During this time, God used my mother to come into my room and anoint my body in preparation for the eulogy of my son.

God prepared me during those nine days so that I could minister to the young men and women who were also mourning my son's death. My faith carried me so that God could use me to help carry others through a difficult time of confusion and anger. My mother informed me after the funeral that my brother Martin recognized God's strength in my weakness. He told my mother, "Ma, Natalie is not human." God gave me the opportunity to eulogize my son and as a result twenty young souls gave their lives to Christ. Patrick did not die in vain because there were souls added to the kingdom. To God be the glory.

Dedication

I would like to acknowledge God, who gave me the strength to retell this story of my past. I dedicate this book in loving memory of my son Patrick H. Felder, and in loving memory of my dear mother Mary J. Reeves. Also, in loving memory of Dr. David L. Tanyhill Jr., who was my son's pastor and played a major role in his spiritual life. To my three beautiful children, Latoya D. Howington, Stephon D. Little, and Joshua B. Ivey, who also loved and cherished their brother and always carried him with them in their heart. I love you. I thank God for providing to you the same strength He provided me as you grieved your brother. To my precious grandchildren: Jamiah Reeves, La' Dia Pitts, Kiara Clemons, and Makai Little, Grandma loves you, and I thank you for being a burst of joy in my life. To my father, Pastor Willie Reeves, thank you for both your love and prayers back then and now. To my siblings Kevin Reeves, Martin Reeves, Wanda Reeves and to my nephew Kevin Reeves Jr., thank you for your love and support. To Anita Williams Blue, Cynthia Dorsey-Wynn and Elise Baker, thank you for covering me during the most difficult time of my life. To Tasha Washington, who helped assist me with this project, and to Patricia Sledge Johnson, thank you for your continuous support and prayers. To my Pastor, Darren L. Duson, thank you for covering me with your prayers, love, support and guidance. To the mothers and fathers who helped give life to these children whose lives were cut short from gun violence, God has a plan for our life. Every high and every low has been orchestrated in ways where God will ultimately get the glory. I also want to take this time to remember the victims and the family members of those who live in Buffalo, NY and Uvalde, Texas. Please accept my heartfelt condolences and know that my prayers are with you during this difficult time of your life. May the God of peace be with you always. Amen.

"The practice of forgiveness is our most important contribution to the healing of the world."

Marianne Williamson

Cecilia M. White, affectionately known as CeCe, is an educator, facilitator, mentor, mother, advocate, and entrepreneur, who currently resides in Valrico, FL. Cecilia was born and raised in Cleveland, Ohio. She has a consultant business that offers services in tutoring, advocacy, and educational services. She has a passion for and a gift that enables her to positively impact the lives of young people. Her involvement in the community demonstrates her commitment to helping society's youth, especially those that have been labeled "at risk".

In prior years she has assisted religious organizations with programs that provide a safe space for children with special needs. Her passions for teaching, writing, and working with those in the special needs community were sparked at a young age. Cecilia continues to serve in her community working with youth as a mentor and advocating for individuals with disabilities.

A BEAUTIFUL BROKEN MASTERPIECE

Cecilia White

The story of my life is that of a beautiful broken masterpiece. I had to understand and see what others saw in me, but more importantly what God sees in me. He created me beautiful. He created me lovely. He created me worthy. He created me in His likeness and image. He created me to be a masterpiece to bring Him glory. I now understand this, but it took a long time to arrive at this understanding. Let's take a journey on how I became a beautiful broken masterpiece.

I have struggled throughout my lifetime trying to figure out who I am, and why me? *Why me?* is a question I often ask myself when I don't understand what's going on in my life. I have repeated cycles of brokenness, guilt, shame, unforgiveness, limited beliefs, condemnation, and much more. Many of these things have played a role like a broken record that keeps skipping and skipping until you lift that needle up and move it over.

I had a beautiful and amazing childhood. My parents made sure I had everything I needed and wanted. I was spoiled by family and friends. I learned to do things and thought I could get away with them, but somehow whatever I did in the dark would come to light. The saying "what you do in the dark will come to light" has become ever so true and real in my life. I was told at a young age, "You can't do wrong and get by, no matter how hard you try." Yeah, I was not one who could do wrong and get by.

I was not allowed to have a boyfriend until I turned eighteen. That was the rule my parents set for me. I attempted to talk to boys from a young age. There was something about a boy that I liked and was interested in. I remember being caught "playing house"—you know, when you role play the mommy and daddy and reenact what you have seen someone else do. Well, this role playing was with the neighbor upstairs. We were around the ages of six and seven, when we were caught kissing by the neighbor next door on the side of the house. I was punished for it and remember being made to sleep in my own bed. I was used to sleeping with my parents every night up until this moment. I felt like my parents rejected me at that time. I didn't know why it was such a bad thing. I was not allowed to talk to boys or be around men.

As a teenager I would sneak and talk to boys, but it seemed that every time I was sneaking to talk to a boy, I would get caught some way or another. My dad was not having it. Whenever I got caught, I would lose my telephone privileges for months at a time. I would still find a way to talk to a boy. What was it about a boy that I felt the need to talk to them despite what my parents required? I remember my first boyfriend at the age of twelve years old. I was caught telling him "I love you" on the telephone and I heard my mother call my name. My heart dropped into my stomach. I knew I was in trouble, but despite the spankings, punishments, and long talks about oil and water not mixing, I still didn't care. I was determined to have a boyfriend.

I remember using my cousins and friends as decoys. I would say I was going to the movies, but who I was at the movies with was nobody's business but my own. I would get my friends and cousins to fabricate their stories with me so none of us would get in trouble. I learned to do this for several years. I thought there was something magical about these boys. I couldn't describe or explain how they made me feel or what the attraction was. I just knew I wanted a boyfriend. Oh, but when I was able to finally have one, with the permission of my parents, it was not what I thought it was. I thought having a relationship with a boy would make me feel like a princess or something. I was wrong. Over the course of my teenage years, I had been with several different guys. I became known as a heartbreaker. I guess some part of me thought it was all right to play with the emotions of these boys and hurt them. As I've reflected on my teenage years, seeing a boy cry because I broke their heart may have been funny to me at that moment, but it sounds crazy now.

Moving forward, as I continued some sort of conquest with a conquer-and-divide mentality, I found myself interested in older men. I was on a search for an experience. What experience was I looking for at the age of seventeen? I started dating a twenty-three-year-old and had a pregnancy scare. I surely didn't know how I was going to go tell my parents that I met a man and now I was pregnant. My parents had high expectations for me. They desired for me to go to school, get a high school diploma, go to college, get a degree, get a good job, get married to a good man, have a good family, and all while living a godly lifestyle in the church.

Well, I did graduate from school and college, I got married, and I was involved heavily in the church. While getting my college degree, I decided to date some older men, and I became very sexually involved with them. I even dated a drug dealer. How did a young girl, born and raised in the church, in a Christian home, end up getting involved with thirty-plus-year-old men and drug dealers? I was on a search for something that I thought they could offer.

I knew I couldn't bring any of these men home to my parents, let alone marry them. I wasn't ready for marriage at all, but at the age of twenty, I knew that I couldn't continue serving God, working in ministry, and living a life of promiscuity.

As I jumped from ministry to ministry, from the ages of fifteen to twenty, I had joined four different churches. That's a story for another day. I asked my dad to release me from going to church with him and for him to allow me to join another church I thought was more fun. I wanted to serve God and have fun. I did just that, although my idea of fun was not being under a microscopic eye of how I was living my life. I could be sneakier, and no one would know. I would say I was on my way to church, but of course I made several stops before arriving to Bible study. I ended up in some crazy places and situations at times, but I believed I was covered.

I remember meeting a young man in one of my religious studies courses. He invited me to come to his church to meet this man he called a prophet. At the time I was in a ministry serving with my friends and dating a guy I thought I was going to marry. He was in the church. I knew I could bring him home to my family. Well, that didn't last long, as I was told that he was not my husband. I walked away from that relationship to find myself in a relationship with a drug dealer. I knew for sure that I was not going to marry this guy nor bring him around my parents. I was told that my husband was in the ministry that I was currently serving in. I started courting my potential husband while dating the drug dealer. I thought I was pregnant by the drug dealer. I had confided in the pastor, who was the father of my potential future husband. He disrespected me so I decided to leave that ministry.

I began visiting the ministry of the prophet. I joined the ministry, but I was still messing with the drug dealer and courting my potential future husband at the same time. I was a mess at twenty years of age. I was told by the prophet that I was in sin and that I needed to get married to get out of sin to avoid going to hell. I got married out of fear. I didn't want to get married to the guy I was courting. I wanted to be with the drug dealer, but I knew that I could not be with him, as he was not in the church and no one in my family would approve of him. So I married the good church guy. I was not the Proverbs 31 woman.

I got married and pregnant all before the age of twenty-one. I was still in college finishing up my bachelor's degree, no job, and volunteering heavily in this new ministry with the prophet. I remember being a few months pregnant and getting into an argument with my husband in my parents' house on a Sunday right before church. My husband punched me so hard in the head, my ear was bleeding. I ran downstairs and grabbed a knife because I was for sure going to kill him right in front of my parents. I didn't know where this rage and anger came from. I was never a violent person, but I was not going to let some man put his hands on me. We became very argumentative toward each other, arguing and fighting, often on the way to church and on the way home. This was the beginning of what continued to be a pattern throughout our relationship.

After my daughter was born, intimacy become nonexistent between my husband and me. I would often fall asleep on the couch while feeding her or end up sleeping in another room. Then I slept in the bed while my husband slept on the floor. Yeah, I didn't want to sleep next to him, with him, or even be near him. I pretended to do what was necessary as a wife while we were at church, but at home I wasn't married. My marriage was only honored at church because I didn't want to have the negative attention and be the highlight of people's conversations. I learned to play the role of a wife and a leader, while despising my marriage the entire time. This is something I learned to do as a teenager, playing the role when it was necessary.

A few months after I graduated college and had my daughter, I had gotten a job as a long-term substitute teacher at a charter school. I met this guy and we became very good friends. I would talk to him about everything. I would spend hours with him. We went to lunch together. I even invited him to church and would pick him up with my husband in the car. Talk about being bold. I had an "I don't care" attitude. I wanted a divorce but getting a divorce would put me in hell, so I stayed in my marriage. I served and volunteered in this same ministry and of course the prophet somehow knew the man I was bringing to church from my job. He called me down to his office to call me out and I denied it. I never slept with the man, but I wanted to. He later passed away, and of course it was the prophet who gave me the news. I was heartbroken. I left that job at the end of the school year.

I was still in the loveless marriage. The stress of unemployment made it harder to be home. When I did find work, it became a place of refuge. Later I found myself attracted to one of my coworkers in whom I also found refuge. We would talk for hours about my life problems. I felt comfortable enough to tell him anything. I began having lustful dreams about and desires for him. Although I was married, I knew that committing adultery with him was also going to send me to hell. I prayed, fasted, spoke to one of the elders in the church, and tried my best to avoid falling into temptation with this coworker. Unfortunately, I found myself committing adultery with him. I lived this double lifestyle of hiding it from my husband and the prophet. Of course, this double lifestyle was something I had learned to do while a teen. I still served in ministry while committing adultery knowingly. I knew I had to tell my husband about the affair. After revealing my truth about the affair, he still wanted to remain married to me. I had a hard time living with this guilt, shame, and condemnation.

I repented and renewed my covenant vows for my ten-year wedding anniversary. That was a fluke because a year later we were separated and found ourselves seeking a marriage counselor to see if we could save our marriage. Well, three years later, we went our separate ways. Now I was no longer in ministry and not abiding by any of the titles I was given while in ministry. I had relocated to Florida. I thought this was my FREEDOM. I started dating, got tatted up, got piercings, was drinking, smoking, and living what I considered my best life. You couldn't tell me anything. I was more concerned about meeting a man or getting into a relationship than I was about my spiritual walk and relationship with God. I was in several toxic, abusive relationships over the course of the next several years. I jumped into a relationship where I could clearly see all the red flags that were there, but I ignored them. He said he believed in God. After dating a few months, I found out that he believed in many things, but not the God I had come to know throughout my life. He was an alcoholic and I suffered mental, physical, verbal, and emotional abuse all over again. I gained the weight that I worked so hard to lose back again. I gained thousands of dollars in debt paying for everything, because I was taking care of him, his child, and my daughter.

My relationship with my daughter struggled during these two years because she didn't want to move in with me. Can you imagine taking care of other people, while your relationship with your own family is suffering? I found myself back in the cycle all over again. The cycle of brokenness, debt, guilt, shame, depression, and abuse was back at my front door. This time, it had a lot of baggage and trash. I prayed and prayed and asked God to get me out of the situation. He simply said, "Walk away, daughter." I stayed two long years and suffered unnecessarily, when all I had to do was walk away. I didn't want to be single or alone. I thought I was going to be lonely. I convinced myself that no one was going to love me and that I was unworthy of receiving the love I so desperately desired, the 1 Corinthians 13 love. I no longer wanted to suffer either, so I decided to finally walk away.

Over the course of the next two years of my life, I was meeting and dating more broken men, men who were abusive and narcissistic. I didn't understand why I kept attracting these types of men into my life, until I realized I was broken. I was in a relationship with another man who I just knew I was going to marry. We didn't have the same views and values in life, but I was set on making it work. Here comes the mental, emotional, verbal, and physical abuse again. I found myself feeling the same way I felt in my marriage and in the previous relationship. I remember taking a trip out of town and we were arguing in the hotel, yelling and screaming. I knew then I had to get out. I had to leave; this was not something I wanted to be in for the remainder of my life.

My relationship with my daughter continued to suffer at the cost of my relationship with men. I neglected to love my daughter and build a relationship with her. I felt like I was the worst mother in the world at times. I knew then that I needed to be a better woman for my daughter. A relationship with a man was not worth losing my relationship with my daughter. After seeking counseling, I was able to repair the relationship with my daughter.

I began asking God, "Where is my husband?" I clearly heard God say, "You'll change your whole life for man, what are you willing to change for me? What are you willing to change in this season?" I had to think about it. I changed jobs, cars, mates, friends, clothes, etc.

If God asks you to change some things in your life in order to receive the promises He has for you, are you willing to do it? Are you going to change those things immediately, over time, or grudgingly? What are you willing to change in this moment?

I had become so broken from past relationships, whether they were romantic, platonic, spiritual, or a friendship. I was searching to fill this void. I was using men as a filler. I was attempting to allow men to fill a void I needed God to fill. I was longing to be accepted by people, but these were the same people who would hurt me. I was searching all over for companionship and using sex as a coping mechanism to deal with the pain and brokenness inside. I found myself turning to God once again, asking Him to help me. I asked, "What am I doing wrong?" He said, "Work on your relationship with me. Get to know me; spend some time with me, let me love you; and show you who are you are to me."

I recommitted my life to the Lord. I'm now somewhere sitting down and working on my relationship with God and with my daughter. I'm no longer chasing men or seeking to be loved by a man. The void I have only God can fix. I'm learning the way God sees me as His daughter and changing how I view Him as my Father. I'm learning to let God love me and fill my heart with love. I'm forgiving myself for not seeing myself as God sees me. I'm forgiving myself for not loving myself and not having the relationship I should with my daughter. I'm forgiving myself for holding on and going back to people and places that are no longer serving me but are keeping me from the will of God. I'm forgiving myself for everything that I've done in my past, as there is no condemnation. I know I am forgiven for my past. I am forgiven and redeemed by God for everything I have done in my past. I'm thankful for the relationship I have with my Heavenly Father today. I am a beautiful broken masterpiece and God is my master of peace.

I will leave you with this love letter I wrote to myself. I recommend if you have an opportunity and some quiet time that you write a love letter to yourself and to God.

Dear Cecilia,

Hey girl, hey. Sis, baby girl, lady, living lady, Proverbs 31 woman, woman of God, God's beautiful daughter, you, my dear, are wonderfully and uniquely made by God your Creator Himself. I want you to know that you are loved, wanted, worthy, enough, and extraordinary. You are favored by God. You are God's favorite. Girl, do you know that loving yourself would bring forth such a beautiful, amazing, joyous, glowing, and transformational experience? Do you know how amazing you are? How resilient you are? How persevering you are? How you walk with grace and ease? You are radiant, extravagant, ravishing, and admirable. You are a whole mood. I want you to know that I love you deeply, wholly, fully, and with all my heart, soul, and mind. I want you to know that you are greatly appreciated. You can do anything you put your mind to. You can do anything you want. You are intentional. You are beautiful, caring, compassionate, generous, bold, gorgeous, sexy, fabulous—all that and so much more. I know you're not perfect. Please stop being so hard on yourself. I know you expect so much of yourself, but show yourself some grace. You have superpowers. You are free to be you. You are growing. The level up is real. Keep going and don't stop. You are transforming into a beautiful woman indeed. Don't be anxious, as everything is working out in God's perfect timing. You must keep trusting that God knows best.

Cecilia, you are more than enough. You are above and not beneath. You are the lender and not the borrower. You are powerful. You are great and mighty. You are a winner. You are chosen. You are divine. You are intelligent, wise, worthy, courageous, strong, and passionate. You have great discernment and judgment. You are triumphant and have overcome so much. You are healthy, happy, and a breath of fresh air. You are refreshing. You matter. You're free, so walk in your freedom and deliverance. You are healed and whole, so walk boldly in your healing. You are complete in God. You are not your past or the things that have happened to you. You are not who you were. You are who God has called and anointed you to be. You are bringing God glory with your life and lifestyle. You are empowered, prosperous, creative, a visionary, growing, learning, living, inventing, unstoppable, inspired, and accomplished. You are a dreamer. You are magnificent. You are the most beautiful person I've ever met. Did I mention, Cecilia, you are beautiful and wonderfully made? Walk boldly in who you are, in whom God made you to be, in whom God called and anointed you to be. I love you for who you are. You don't look like what you've been through. Continue to let every step you take move you forward toward God's promises for you, and don't look back. You got this, Sis. You are saved and redeemed. You are a beautiful broken masterpiece that has now been made whole.

Love Always,
Cecilia M. White

Ms. Antionette Dominique Washington is a proud native of New Orleans, LA. She is also an alumnus of Jackson State University. In 2014, she received her Bachelor's in Social Work. and in 2018, she received her Master's in Social Work. In addition, Antionette has been accepted by Tulane University in pursuit of her Doctorate in Social Work.

She relocated to Georgia seeking better opportunities for her family and career. She is currently an author, entrepreneur, and mother of twin boys. In her spare time, she teaches her sons the importance of education and accomplishing goals. For that reason, Antionette is currently developing the blueprint for her own private practice "HER Therapeutic Breakthrough".

Antionette has been working as an active social worker for seven years. She has a passion for mentoring adolescents. She believes the up-and-coming generations need proper guidance and positive roles models. As a result, she has served as a big sister with the Big Brother/Big Sister organization (Jackson, MS), and a mentor for Archdiocese (New Orleans, LA). She is also working with individuals with Intellectual Developmental Disabilities in Georgia and its surrounding areas.

AFTER THE STORM – I AM HER

Antoinette D. Washington

My messes have become my message, my tests have become my testimony and my pain has become my gain. I have had to learn how to activate my faith and deactivate my fear. I once lived in fear; it kept me going in circles and confused. It is easy and often inherited to inflict self-blame after experiencing trauma from those you trusted most and never expected to hurt you. I have experienced trauma spiritually, mentally, emotionally, physically, financially, and sexually from family, friends and men. Trusting the process and believing in God has carried me through every traumatic experience I have ever endured. It has not been an easy journey, nor has it always been pleasurable, but it has been one that has taught me patience, forgiveness, and gratitude.

I have cried and prayed many nights with the questions why, when, where, and how, still not understanding how to properly heal from my traumas. I was not provided a guide on how to heal. I had to first understand that I needed to release in order to receive what I needed, what I wanted and what God had for me. I had become my own worst enemy and was standing in the way of my own elevation, healing and growth. I decided to be transparent with myself and be like NIKE: "Just Do It." I decided to just start the journey with an open heart and an open mind. I began doing the work internally first, then externally. It was time to take control of my life and live it, not allow my past to dictate my future but to allow my past to shape my future. It was long overdue that I stop hiding in the shadows of what others thought of me and had projected on me, but to hold my head high, know who the heck I am and that whatever I do moving forward, I do it with a purpose. I am authentically and unapologetically me.

Everyone has their own definition of what trauma means to them, how they stepped out on faith, what methods they used to gain survivorship and how they refused to give up. Reflecting on the things I have been through and what I did to survive has humbled me in more ways than I can count. I will share a few of my traumatic events and how I had to step out on faith and trust in the process, knowing God would get me through.

One, this is the most sensitive and most affecting trauma I have experienced. Both of my parents had their choice of drugs that allowed them to neglect and abuse me in different ways. My father, who is now deceased, was a crack and alcohol abuser. He loved me dearly and made sure everyone knew it, but his extracurricular activities were a priority over me. There were times when he tried to balance us all but there was no room for me to compete with the two. They won every time until he decided to gain and maintain sobriety. I witnessed him getting high and drunk; I sat on the steps of crack houses in the lower ninth ward across the canal while he decided to get his fix. Before his passing he and I often laughed at how he once got so drunk he left my backpack on the city bus. All he could say was, "Ah girl, now I gotta deal with your momma and her crazy-ass shit." If I shared how old I was when these events occurred it would blow your mind, especially knowing that I recall those events like they were yesterday. For those who knew my father, they know his mouth was reckless and could not be filtered. His words did not discriminate against age or gender; anyone could get it. Despite his mouth, he was cool, laid back, loving and could make you laugh. Due to his spiraling drug and alcohol addiction my grandfather "Pawpaw" purchased my dad a one-way ticket to Hawaii to get him out the city before someone decided to harm him. I could not have been happier; I was living in Hawaii being raised by my aunt, so I was excited and was looking forward to my dad being a part of my life again. Well, it was not long after being in a foreign place that he connected with locals who shared the same interest as him and he was back to his usual. It hurt knowing so young that he was on drugs, but I never viewed him as less than my dad. I valued the quality time he invested in me and it always felt comforting hearing "I love you, Apple Head" even when he was high and drunk. There was never a time he didn't say those words to me.

I thought I healed the day he asked for forgiveness. I forgave him but I was far from healed. I was too young and did not know how to properly heal. I simply appreciated the apology and acknowledgement. Once he made up in his mind sobriety was a priority overall, I received a dad I had never had. I was happy.

Due to my continuous back-and-forth from living with different people, there were periods of time where my dad and I were apart but the love was never lost. Early on, my dad always wanted the best for me. He wanted me to be different by applying myself and making better choices. Due to him barely being able to read and write, he wanted me to get a good education. In return, I did just that. I graduated high school and received my Bachelor's and Master's. Even though my dad's health was declining during those special accomplishments, he made sure to muscle up the strength to be in attendance. By accomplishing those goals, I made him smile, but for me to have him witness them with me meant even more. There is nothing that can replace those feelings. In contrast, accomplishing those goals helped me heal from the traumas I experienced with him, and I was able to release what no longer existed.

After my dad's health transitioned and swiftly declined even more, I made the decision to move me and my boys back home to New Orleans to care for him. Reflections made me mentally and emotionally abuse myself. I felt guilty for not being in a position to care for him full time. I was raising my twin boys, pursuing my degree, going through an ugly divorce and working three jobs. Yet he always expressed how he was grateful for everything my boys and I did for him up to his passing. Daily I was at the hospital, sometimes three times a day. I made sure I was there every step of the way until I placed that last kiss on his forehead and released his hand. Seeing the pain in his eyes, that last breath did something to me inside. A part of me was gone and it felt so sudden.

Sadly, I now reminisce over the memories we shared, from our tears and conversations to the bond shared between him and my boys. Trust me, I know I did my part as his daughter, with love, compassion, strength and gratitude. I have no regrets. As I look back, I am so proud of the choices he made to get back on track. His sobriety taught me to have faith, believe in myself, and that nothing is too big to accomplish. I know he is proud; I survived unexpected events, I didn't become a victim of my environment, and I never gave up. Finally, I am thriving. I have been receiving and will continue to receive what the universe has for me.

I will always love you, Dad ~Apple Head.

Second, my mom...I have to laugh, smile and shake my head as I share this traumatic story. My mom is a character and a hot mess. I say that with love and pure honesty. As I stated earlier, my mom had her choice of drug too. Her choice of drug and priority has always been men. My mom never raised me; she barely knows me and today our relationship remains stagnant and strained. It took me years to admit what I did not want to accept. I knew early on my mom never wanted me and did not like me. Her hate toward my dad was so strong she allowed it to cause her to neglect and abuse me. I never received motherly love. Acceptance day scared me and caused me to build a wall of what I thought was protection but more like subjection to fear, discomfort, and anger inheritance. My grandmother would sit in her bedroom crying while I had my bags packed and stood at the front door waiting on her to pick me up for the weekend. You can only imagine the disappointment and hurt when time after time I was told to close the door after hours had gone by and I was still waiting.

I was hoping, wishing and praying she would come for me, yet another broken promise. My grandmother had cried herself out, and she finally sat me down and told the truth: that my mom did not want to be bothered. She let me know she was not coming. That very moment did something to me. I knew what was being shared was true but I did not want to hear it or receive it. Consciously I had already accepted what was factual but the rest of my subconscious was staggering behind because that little girl in me wanted that motherly love. I was fortunate enough to have relatives intervene and take me under their wing in support of my grandmother and to fill my empty void. It is appreciated and played a significant role in my life, but I still yearned for the attention, affection, and so much more from my mom.

I can recall being left on the steps of Oakbrook apartments and was told, "Yo daddy and pawpaw is on their way; just wait here for them." Yes, she left and went off with her African boyfriend "Oochie." I remember I didn't like him and neither did anyone else. He was an opportunist, receiving what he wanted every time he was granted access. He never had intentions of settling down with her; he was just in it for the moment. To my rescue like always, one if not both always showed up without a doubt. I remember the anger and pain in my dad's and grandfather's eyes. I witnessed multiple men in and out of her life. Like the old school saying, she changed men more than she changed her panties. She was never embarrassed or saw how she was disrespecting her own self. I was always embarrassed by her behavior and obsession with chasing a man. I always said that would never be me.

The abuse continued; there were multiple occasions even the few times I did actually live with her and of course, the countless number of times I was not living with her. There was this one time when she was dating this bald mouthed man who she was so crazy over, just to say she had a man. He and I got off to a rough start, and I mean rough. It was so rough and uncomfortable my friend and I at the time strongly considered poisoning him. Yeah, when you are young but severely hurting, you are impulsive at times. You act or attempt to act without carefully considering the consequences. A plan and call were in effect but God has a way of handling things better than we do. He and I exchanged ugly words one night and as I was on my way out, my ride arrived, and before I could get in the car, she jumped on me from behind and was hitting me nonstop. I attempted to hit her back in defense but a voice yelled out, "You better not." They did not like or agree with what was happening but I guess it was the principle for them behind a daughter hitting her mom back. Time passed and bald mouth and I developed a relationship. The physical abuse from my mom was not often but that did not stop the mental, emotional or financial abuse from recurring.

Back in the day she was laid and paid, a frequent flyer in the hair salon and nail shop—so often, regular was an understatement. I, on the other hand, was a bald-headed tag-along. I did not know what it was like to sit alongside my mom and get my hair done. She combed my hair herself when she felt like it. My big cousin Lisa took me under her wing and gave me the exposure and experience of being pampered. But the embarrassment just continued growing. My school shoes were my weekend shoes. I will never forget them, white "g niks" with the orange bubble. Of course, they did not match my school uniform, but she was not pressed or stressed. The other children would "rib" me often, outside New Orleans terminology, "tease me." I was so tired of the neglect and being an outsider. My mom always spent money on herself and, of course, the man she was with at the time, but not me.

I decided to ask my eighth-grade boyfriend at the time to put me on. What did I know about selling drugs? Absolutely nothing, but I had a resource and access to easy money. Again, God had a way of intervening and letting me know my plan was not his plan. Between Avondale, the 9th ward, her best friend, coworkers, my Paperanian and anyone else who could keep me for her to run the streets and be with a man was her thing. I had become so immune to it, it no longer bothered me as long as she was coming to get me. But her pattern remained consistent and her feelings never changed toward me. I was a burden and she did not care to be bothered with me.

Hurricane Katrina hit, and she was forced to relocate. She received a transfer from her job and was working at the VA in Long Beach, California. I was left behind at a private boarding school I was attending in Mississippi. I was content, but shortly after returning to school from California myself, I was expelled. Again, she did not want me there with her; her excuse this time was she was residing in a hotel. My grandmother did not want the responsibility, nor did she want me back in New Orleans. So off to Long Beach I went. Well, to my surprise and hers as well, she received a call, one she had been hoping for. The VA in New Orleans was opening back up and wanted her back. She did her usual, neglecting her only child. She packed her bags and left. I was left behind to live with my uncle. Again, I faced the hurt, the pain, the feeling of knowing I was not important enough for her to stay or for me to go. My uncle and I did not have much of a relationship; it was like living with a known stranger. I wanted to stay at the school in Long Beach, where I had gained friends. Due to me begging and pleading, my uncle finally agreed to let me finish school in Long Beach. I was catching two busses to get back and forth to school, an hour ride each way because of the new distance. The commute was foreign and scary but I did what I had to do. Some nights I was getting home late due to night school. Rides were not often from my uncle. Survival was real, but I have no regrets. I wanted to continue attending school where it was diverse over attending school where he worked. The school was predominantly white and wealthy, a school I was not interested in attending.

There was so much built-up pain and anger I carried for years that it delayed my elevation. I believed my trauma was normal. I ignored red flags, made excuses, survived on justifications. I had become the mess. My families' continuous judgmental statements never made it any better. I could not breathe; I could not see, hear nor think straight. I was just existing in ongoing traffic with no warning signs.

Giving birth was a reminder of who I did not want to become and the things I never wanted to subject my children to. I made a promise to myself to always love and protect my children. I stand on that promise today. Being a parent has its challenges, especially being a single mother to twin boys. I have had to grow up a lot, make sacrifices, and think critically about things I was not ready for. However, it has taught me the value of needing to heal and grow on different levels in life so I can be a better woman, a better mother, not just for them but for myself.

October 2020 was the beginning for me. My mind shifted and was made up to do something about the things I was sick and tired of – toxic relationships, the going in circles, the abuse from those in my circle, the not prioritizing, self-doubt, insecurities of failing. Fear consumed me and my mind frame had become impoverished.

I started looking for a therapist. I decided it was time to see a professional to let go of my past, address what was going on in my present and start preparing for a healthier future. I gained a therapist and was on my new journey—well, at least I thought so. COVID interrupted my services. I attempted to restart services several times with that particular therapist, but I really wanted an African American female who I felt could relate a little more. I received what I manifested a year later. I found a dope Black therapist. I decided to give this therapy thing a try again.

Sessions began shortly after reaching out to her, and it was well worth it. I was being held accountable for my choices. I was challenged to think and be transparent with myself and assigned homework. She is professional, compassionate and understanding, exactly what I needed. The journey was just beginning. I was now facing multiple tests that I did not expect. My faith, strength, and wisdom were tested on different levels. I was truly transitioning. Some tests I failed and had to retake; some I passed. The biggest test was trusting the process, letting go of what I could not control.

Family can be a mess. You love them, but they can do and say things that make you dislike them. I was residing in a family home after my dad passed. My grandmother's friend/over-involver convinced my grandmother to move out of her family home and move into an assisted living facility. My grandmother followed suit. I was asked, practically convinced, to move in the house. I moved in for several different reasons, but I was not expecting to be evicted via text by the over-involver. I was notified in July and was expected to evacuate immediately. The situation grew ugly, and the courts became involved. Furthermore, I was fired from my job after being bullied and retaliated against. So I had no income and was looking for a place to stay. Back to the drawing board. My faith was put to the test more than ever. Humiliation, anger, and fear were starting to grow inside me like a cancer I could not cure.

I decided to pray, manifest and seek clarification. I decided it was long overdue to receive bigger and better. I made an easy decision to start looking for jobs in my field but outside of New Orleans. I was ready to take a leap of faith and do what I had been wanting to do for years—move to Atlanta. But before I did, I needed to clean house where I was so I could move forward as a better version of myself. I had one last test to pass, one I was not sure if I was ready.

I never thought I would be asking my mom if my children and I could live with her temporarily until I relocated. I had not lived with my mom in over fifteen years. God has a way of humbling you. I knew I had to pass this test, and it was not going to be an easy one. There was pride and animosity built up, but I put it to the side, thinking about my children and what was ahead for us. Two months was the time frame we stayed with my mom; a lot occurred in that short period of time.

Therapy and the simple decision to choose my peace and happiness over her toxic ways were far more valuable than allowing her spirit to disturb my energy and interrupt my peace. I made a decision to stop trying to control what I could not control and take responsibility for my responses and reactions toward her. It was not easy, but I stayed focused on what was important, which was to get to where my children and I needed to be. Arguments occurred, comments were passed, but I no longer reacted in defense; however, I responded. I responded with facts, grace and humbleness. She would be in a yelling match with herself.

I decided to apply for jobs much sooner than I originally stated I would. I filled out two applications in December but felt that was not good enough. I decided to stop playing and do what I knew needed to be done: fill out applications consistently. I was guided and led by spirit to stop postponing and making excuses for trying to stay behind longer than needed. I trusted the process and took a chance on myself. I listened, thankfully. I was offered a job in January. I officially started on February 14 and was in Georgia by February 28.

Before leaving home all I wanted was for my babies to experience marching in the parade with their school before relocating. We were given that opportunity. I knew at that moment I could breathe, smile and let go. The three of us were so ready to leave. We left after a full two days of marching in parades. The clock read 2:22AM. We had arrived. A new chapter was established.

Living with my mom opened my mind as a professional social worker and as her daughter. I grew to understand that she was mentally disturbed and there was a competency blockage. She does not accept the neglect or abuse and pain she inflicted on me as a child and young adult because in her mind she did not do it. I had to understand that she has selective memory when it is convenient for her. Addressing sensitive matters with her during the two months I was staying there, I observed and realized it was like talking to a client at times. The understanding is limited, and she could not acknowledge her wrongs because she had not yet accepted them. Accountability and responsibility are not on her side. I have accepted that I may never get my questions answered and she may never change.

During that time I decided I would no longer allow her wrongs to affect me and my future. I released every painful, toxic, unhealthy association that I have ever had with her. I love her but I have set boundaries and will protect my peace and energy by any means necessary. I deal with my mom on my terms and in my way. I am not wiling to lose the healing, happiness and growth that I have worked hard for.

Many ask me how I do it. Looking back at what I have been through, where I am now compared to where I am headed, I smile and share, the recipe is easy but staying consistent is the ultimate test. Raw uncut honesty: I decided I was tired of my messes, my stressors, and my traumas controlling me. First things first: I took accountability for what I could not control and accepted that change was needed to better myself as a woman first. I started listening to morning affirmations, journaling, meditating, manifesting, and going to weekly therapy.

That was just the beginning. I had to shift my mind frame, the way I think, the company I keep, the things I speak into my life. I was willing to remove whoever no longer belonged in my life and whatever no longer needed to be in my life. It is hard and a challenge letting go, but the peace and clarity it brings makes up for the loss and pain. I have learned everyone is not deserving of my time and energy. It was time to start receiving positive deposits, not withdrawals and no negativity. They can save the continuous withdrawals and constant overdrafts for their bank. I'm not the one, two or three. I no longer play about me, and I will no longer allow others to play with me either. Boundaries are a must in my life to maintain the healed version of myself as I continue to grow and go forward.

~ I am her; she is me; we are one.

Dedication

I dedicate this chapter to my self-awareness, my growth, and my progress. I am so hard on myself most days and I often find myself struggling with toasting to my accomplishments, complimenting myself and having gratitude for my successes. Some may say its selfish but as women we need to prioritize celebrating ourselves more. I dedicate this chapter to closing old chapters in my life, healing old wounds, and releasing what and who no longer serves me. Why not now... This is that moment where I toast to my accomplishment and celebrate me. God has blessed me with an opportunity I am so proud to be able to partake in. I am humbly grateful. I toast to me in the now and to all my future successes.

Tymesha Renee Sene was born and raised in Denver, Colorado. Now living in Delaware, Ohio, she is married to her best friend and amazing husband. She is the proud mom to her beautiful and vibrant miracle daughter. Tymesha is a minister and anointed worshipper that God has gifted to set atmospheres through prophetic song and dance. She is currently in the process of creating a prophetic flow CD that she hopes to release next year.

Tymesha is part of an amazing non-profit organization and is also an entrepreneur who loves to empower and equip women to create residual income through network marketing. Because she is a lifelong learner, she recently became a John Maxwell certified speaker, trainer and coach and has participated in several masterminds, increasing her personal growth and helping her gain a better understanding of how to connect and communicate effectively in her spheres of influence.

HEALED AS THEY WENT
A Journey of Healing One Step at A Time

Tymesha Gene

I begin my story by referring to a familiar passage of scripture in Luke 17:13-19, KJV: "And they lifted their voices, and said, Jesus, Master, have mercy on us. And when he saw them, he said unto them, Go shew yourselves unto the priests. And it came to pass, that, as they went, they were cleansed. And one of them, when he saw that he was healed, turned back, and with a loud voice glorified God, And fell down on his face at his feet, giving him thanks: and he was a Samaritan. And Jesus answering said, were there not ten cleansed? but where are the nine? There are not found that returned to give glory to God, save this stranger. And he said unto him, Arise, go thy way: thy faith hath made thee whole."

I want to take some time to unpack these verses and how they relate to my journey of healing. Note that when the lepers lifted their voices and cried out to Jesus to have mercy on them, when he saw them, he did not lay hands on them; he did not pray for them for hours; he simply said "go and show": go and show yourself unto the priest and as they went, they were healed. Not when they finally "arrived," but as they were going, as they were being obedient and simply obeying instructions. When the Lord impressed upon my heart a few years ago to share my story, I wasn't only shocked but utterly terrified. Though I've had confirmation upon confirmation that there was a book in me, never would I have taken it upon myself to share my pain with the masses, so believe me when I say this is under the unction of the Holy Spirit. Stepping into purpose takes courage and an unyielding *yes* as you go through the vicissitudes of life. There are times when God will speak a word, the heavens will open and the Sprit will descend upon you strongly, and you'll think you're ready to run with the vision and word he gave you, only to be driven into a wilderness, isolated and fighting with the adversary whose purpose is to steal, kill and destroy you and your destiny and calling.

Like Jesus in the wilderness, isolation trains you for faithfulness, and your faithfulness decides God's divine timing. When I speak of isolation, I'm not referring to avoiding people; I've been in crowds and felt isolated. No, I'm referring to the tiny little cage you run to in your mind that shuts you off mentally from the rest of the world, that place where the enemy meets you with popcorn and candy and reruns the reel of your past repeatedly in 3D, whispering in your ear, "You'll never amount to anything; no one is ever going to love you, you're broken, you're too old, too fat, too skinny, not attractive"—the list goes on and on. He'll taunt you and convey all the reasons why you should give up. I've lived in that isolated place in my head for years and if it had not been for the Lord who was on my side, I really don't know where I would be. One thing I can say is that during the chaos of my life God's favor has followed me down through the years in many areas. I haven't been perfect, but I have been faithful, and I've had to trust the process, a process I didn't even realize I was in until the Holy Spirit began kicking the crutches out from under me and forcing me to face me. As I mentioned before, faithfulness decides divine timing and my time is now, and if you are reading this, your divine timing is now! I don't understand the road traveled to get to this point, but I'm embracing it all and that has helped me to do the inner work and to be vulnerable and give myself permission to share my story from a place of authenticity rather than spuriousness, transparency rather than ambiguity, and from a better place not a bitter place, from a victim to a victor. So here we go.

I was born in 1972 and raised in Denver, Colorado. Due to dissociative amnesia, it is difficult for me to recall many memories from my childhood, but I would say I was happy and full of hopes and dreams like most girls. I dreamed of being swept away by Prince Charming, having an elaborate wedding, a big house with a white picket fence, and running a Fortune 500 company. Right at the moment when this little flower was beginning to feel the refreshing dew of life, stretching its petals toward the sun ready to blossom, those dreams turned into nightmares within a few moments in time, and my world came crashing down around me. I was molested and emotionally abused by my father from age 11 through my teenage years. This set me on a path of psychological torment for years to come. No longer was I happy and free, but I felt dirty and worthless. My entire life seemed like a stage play, and I was forced into the role and character of a script that couldn't have been written for me. This was not what I envisioned when I played with my dolls, giving them all happily-ever-afters. Speaking of dolls, there was Baby Chrissy, who according to my mother I had a love/hate relationship with. Baby Chrissy had a little ring in her back, which allowed me to lengthen or shorten her hair at will. Something about that freaked me out and made me mad. I believe even then the prophetic was working in me and she represented what my hair dilemma would look like in the years to come, but I digress; that is another chapter. Feeling as if the oxygen had been sucked out of my life, there weren't many joyous days that I looked forward to. I didn't enjoy school because there was no reprieve for me there either.

I rarely had the opportunity to enjoy normal experiences like most kids growing up. There were no proms, homecoming dances, attendance at pep rallies and high school games. He controlled every area of my life. If I was allowed to participate in anything, it was under strict management where school functions, outings with friends, and family were concerned. Participating in anything that involved crowds made me nervous and anxious because if I was caught glancing at a boy or they said hi to me, it led to a criminal interrogation or worse, so most of the time I walked around with my head down.

Anyone who knows me knows I love to sing, and I remember trying out for a girl's ensemble and I made the cut. I was so excited, but when it came time for us to perform at the weekend competition in another city, which required an overnight stay, I was forbidden to go. I was devastated and heartbroken. It was at that moment that I lost any aspiration for my studies, and I realized how small my world had become. There were times I would come out of class and see my father roaming the hallway, and my heart felt like it would leap out of my chest. You may be asking why I didn't say something to anyone. How could I let this go on for so long? What do you do when you are told that access to you would keep your family together? Imagine carrying around that burden, wanting out but not wanting to hurt your family. The bright, smart, talented girl was now afraid, living in a shell, ridden with guilt, shame, and heartache. I learned how to live behind a mask, which was exhausting and depressing. Lonely and frustrated, feeling imprisoned in my mind, body and soul, there were many times I wished for death. I attempted suicide, cutting my wrists and popping pills; I contemplated running away on a few occasions but the fear of being hurt on the street seemed scarier than being hurt at home. Arrested in my development, I always felt awkward, like a misfit, inferior, so I spent my life striving to be more, do more, and prove to myself and to others that I was worthy and valuable. Having a poor self-image and always feeling insecure kept me from living the vibrant, fearless, intentional life I was created to live. This affected me tremendously, sending me down a path of bad relationships, failed marriages, missed opportunities, and making life-altering decisions from a shame-based mentality. But I thank God that he never stopped looking upon me when I cried out with a loud voice, and sharing this story is His command to "go and show yourself." Being transparent about your pain is often the promotion to your next level. The journey of becoming the best version of who God has called you to be will force you to open your heart and unpack your baggage. I am overwhelmed with a myriad of emotion and cleansing tears that have been shed, and the shackles that have fallen off my mind have been life transformational. As I continue to take the steps toward my healing, I feel a renewed strength, zeal for life, fearlessness and boldness taking place in the deep recesses of my being. By the stripes of Jesus Christ, we are healed, but it is by faith that we walk toward that healing, walk toward being our authentic selves, operating in the unique purpose and destiny that God has designed for us.

Navigating through all the self-sabotaging systems engrained in me, I always felt a deep call on my life. I accepted the Lord at an early age, and I grew up in church serving the Lord, so I knew Him, I just didn't know what He was doing with me. Surely my life was meant for more than what I was experiencing. The blunders of my life have often put me on display like a tourist attraction and discovering who I am has been agonizing and refreshing at the same time. I feel like God certainly could have sped up this revelatory moment but now I realize that I'm where I'm supposed to be exactly at this time. Yes, you read it right! Recognize that every experience—the good, the bad and the ugly—plays a vital part in growth and healing. Before I was created, the Lord knew me. He's known every mistake, every tear, every heartbreak, every disappointment, every messy situation. Jeremiah 1:5 says, "Before I formed you, I knew you, set you apart." God knows the thoughts he has for you, and they are peaceful; they are plans to prosper you not to harm you, give you a hope and a future (Jeremiah 29:11-13). So, no matter where you may be right now, know that your expected end is in his hands, and he has faith in you to be who he has called you to be. The path to get there will be filled with winding roads, hills, valleys, roadblocks, and detours and will be under construction at times but keep trusting God and celebrate the progress along the way, no matter how insignificant you think it is. It wasn't until I stopped striving and began to rest in who I am that I understood the beauty and the peace of being comfortable in the skin you're in. No matter what your life may throw your way and how bad you fumble the play, God doesn't change His mind about you. Wherever you go, whatever you're doing or have done, the blueprint for your life remains the same, and it is your responsibility to take those plans and partner with the Chief Architect (the Holy Spirit) and allow him to demolish fear, guilt, shame and doubt and uncover the foundation built on the original plan God has for your life. "You are fearfully and wonderfully made" (Psalm 139:14).

Friend, I can tell you that healing from trauma of any kind isn't easy, but it is attainable. You must face the pain. You can't manage what you can't confront, so it's time to stop running from it and run toward it with everything you've got and cut off its head. In 1 Samuel 17 we read the story of David and Goliath. Goliath taunted Saul and the Israelites for forty days, daring them to send a man to fight, defying their army. That is what the enemy likes to do; he's been taunting you for years, daring you to stand up and fight. The Bible says that Saul and the Israelites were dismayed and terrified, yet they did nothing. Ask yourself, "What am I allowing to terrify me and how long will I allow it to rob me of an abundant, healthy, fruitful life?" Whatever it is; God desires you to be free and walk in victory. When David told Saul he would go and fight Goliath, Saul told him he was too young so David whipped out his resume, then Saul dressed him in his tunic and helmet, but David couldn't function in Saul's armor. Verse 39 in the King James Version says, David assayed to go because he had not proved the armor. When you prepare to go into battle to fight your Goliath for your healing process, prove everything. You'll have things put on you that won't fit and will try to hinder you from being free to face your giants. The Spirit of God will lead you into all truth, just trust that God has equipped you with everything you need to fight your adversary. The longer you carry the weight of your pain and trauma, the weaker you will become. It will deplete your energy, joy, peace, and happiness.

I've not arrived at the totality of my healing. There are good days and challenging days, and I fight to walk in my wholeness daily. However, what I have truly arrived at is that I am worthy of love, respect, and honor and that I am more than enough and can take my seat at the table the Lord has prepared for me. The Passion translation of Romans 8:38-39 reads, "So now I live with the confidence that there is nothing in the universe with the power to separate us from God's love. I'm convinced that his love will triumph over death, life's troubles, fallen angels, or dark rulers in the heavens. There is nothing in our present or future circumstances that can weaken his love. There is no power above us or beneath us—no power that could ever be found in the universe that can distance us from God's passionate love, which is lavished upon us through our Lord Jesus, the Anointed One!" Wow. God wants to lavish his love on us as his daughters and he is longing for us to take our rightful places in the kingdom. Because I knew man's "love" from a distorted, perverted and dysfunctional viewpoint before I had a chance to know God's love, it took me a long time to understand the magnitude and weight of this verse. The purity, beauty, innocence, and magnificence of God's love was incomprehensible. I equated serving and living for Him with fear, intimidation, manipulation, and control. Unconditional, unwavering, unmerited love of God? I could never fathom God loving me like that, not with all these ugly scars. It's just like the enemy to make you think that Christ shedding his blood and being the propitiation for the sins of the whole world somehow didn't include you. Imagine that. Our Heavenly Father loves us just as we are. Isaiah 43:1, NKJV says, "But now, thus says the LORD, who created you, O Jacob, And He who formed you, O Israel: 'Fear not, for I have redeemed you; I have called you by your name; You are Mine.'" Your name is special to God. The enemy will always call you by your sin, your past, your history, but the Lord calls you by your name. He calls you daughter, he calls you royal priesthood, he calls you blessed and highly favored. And once you recognize your name, you'll stop answering to any other name. God sent his only Son to die so that you and I could have eternal life, an abundant life here right now, not in the sweet by and by but right now. Embrace the love God has for you, a love you don't have to strive for, a love that will change your life and give you a freedom to just be. Just as salvation is a process—you're saved, you're being saved and you shall be saved—the healing process works the same way: you are healed, being healed and you shall be healed. Luke 11:24-25 says, "When an unclean spirit comes out of a man, it passes through arid places seeking rest and does not find it. Then it says, I will return to the house I left and, on its return, finds the house swept clean and put in order. Then it goes and brings seven other spirits more wicked than itself, and they go in and dwell there and the final plight of that man is worse than the first." Every level of victory in your healing journey will require you to protect the boundaries of the territory you gain because the enemy will never just leave you alone. He will bring reinforcements to attack you. He'll use people, circumstances, occasional trips down memory lane that pick at your scabs—anything to find a kink in your armor. Every day I wake up I choose to walk in a place of peace, healing, love, and value. I choose to show up for myself, my family and all those connected to me. I choose to reveal my scars as I continue to grow and have the broken pieces of my life mended by God. So dear reader, if you have been crying out to the Lord in your situation, he is telling you to get up and go shew yourself and as you trust Him and take those crucial steps, just as I did, one day you will be going along and recognize that you have been made whole. You will finally see you beyond the pain – beautiful, gifted, unique, valuable and authentic. When you are healed and delivered, praise God with a loud voice, throw yourself at his feet and give him thanks. And every day decide to rise and go because your faith has made you whole.

    I want to thank my Lord and Savior Jesus Christ for all things, my family, friends, and those who have been in the trenches with me or watched and cheered for me from the sidelines. Thanks to my wonderful husband for his unwavering love, support, and patience; and for loving me past my pain and allowing me space and grace to grow and blossom, and to my amazing daughter, who inspires me every day to live life to the fullest and to show up whole every day. Last but certainly not least, a special thanks to the visionary ArDenay Garner for the opportunity to co-author with some amazing women on this anthology. We are "Resilient Black Women Shaping the World with our Faith," and I am truly honored.

Robin Young, 46 years old, was born and raised in Windy City Chicago, IL.

In 1993 Robin enlisted in the United States Navy at 18 and was one of the first 500 women to go out to sea with men on a Naval Air-Craft Carrier USS Eisenhower in the field of aviation. She has been a successful salon owner and serial entrepreneur for over 24 years. She has two beautiful children, Christian, 26 and Jonathan 16. She is married to her wonderland husband Mark David Young. They reside in Jacksonville, Florida. Robin and Mark have a successful Basketball Post Grad Academy and they have helped send more than 17 young Black men to college.

Robin has always had a heart for people and serving her community. She has served our country, ministry, and community for over 20 years. She is an extraordinary leader and example to women. Her courage, wisdom, and relentless drive to face life's challenges head on, has allowed her to excel in every area of her life. She takes pride in helping women find their purpose in business and spiritual endeavors. Robin believes that "When you know your passion you will find your purpose".

YOUR PURPOSE WILL FIND YOU

Robin Young

As I looked through the window of our first-floor apartment on the Chicago Southside, I was only 15 years old. I saw the most beautiful woman in the world to me put the poison to her mouth, and I knew at that moment I was on my own. I sat there staring at my mother, not knowing then how young she was and the pain that she must have had inside that caused her to do a drug that had claimed so many lives in the place we called "The Hood." As I stared at her with pain and disappointment in my eyes, I didn't know how much she needed to be loved. All I could do was feel a sense of terror rush through my body, a sense of abandonment, loss and rejection. You see...cocaine was the thing that took my mother far away from me. My mother was only 15 years old when she gave birth to me. She was a product of her environment and she didn't realize how beautiful she was to me, that I needed her to be my mother and my example. She obviously had so much pain inside and was drowning in her own story, she couldn't be what I needed her to be to me. The poison of cocaine became her outlet that ultimately blinded her from seeing her value and her worth.

All I could do is think about the way I felt that day, and I knew it was gonna be me against the world. I became overwhelmed with emotion. I knew I had to do anything necessary to escape the inevitable curse that society had put on little black girls. Both of my parents were addicted to crack Cocaine and living in the ghetto, which put a stamp of automatic failure on my life. But I decided to get out and change the narrative. That day shaped my future and the path that would ultimately cultivate me into becoming a strong and resilient woman. But make no mistake, it would be a path of tremendous inner pain.

My mother was the steppingstone to my inner strength. She represented what people set as a marker for who and what my future would be. I had to prove them wrong and shut up every demon in hell. I had to become a woman who didn't have a statistic on her life of teenage pregnancy, drug addiction and low self-esteem. Little did I know I was in for some difficult times ahead that would challenge my way of thinking and the very core of my being.

That summer was the hardest summer of my life. It was also the summer I lost my innocence. Then I was up against myself and my own mistakes. My first experience was with a jealous and abusive young man. We had so many fights, and I thought this was normal and I was in love. Oh boy, was I wrong. Because I didn't have an example of a healthy relationship and neither did he, we were young and full of untamed emotions. In some way I was attracted to the dysfunction of it all, because I didn't know how a young man should treat me or what was acceptable. This was not good at all. It had gotten so bad that I decided to end the relationship and he was furious. I remember our mutual friend calling me, saying, "Robin, please don't go over to his house tonight because he has created a noose and he is planning to kill you and hang you in his basement. My mother must have felt something terrible was going to happen that day because she said to me out of nowhere, "Boobie (my nickname), don't go over that boy's house today." I thought to myself she must have known that I was in grave danger. Looking back on that time, I know God had His hand on my life because not even two years later he became addicted to drugs as well.

Abuse comes in many forms. Abusers can wear many disguises. But let's be very clear; there is a saying that says, "You teach people how to treat you." That relationship set the tone for my life that would shape the way I felt about men and how I would allow men to perceive me, especially when I said the three magic words to them, "I LOVE YOU." Looking back on that time, I didn't realize that I was codependent. I would carry this trait with me for many years and sabotage myself over and over, because I didn't want to feel the rejection and abandonment I felt the night I saw my mother put the poison to her mouth. So I became "the get-along gang member." I would do things to please my man, even when I didn't want to, because I didn't want to be abandoned. I would soon walk in this attribute of codependency in my first marriage, which caused me much pain but taught me many things about myself. One thing I know for sure is God was with me every turn and captured every tear. Here's where we will take a praise break.

The enemy tried to throw his curse on me at 15 years old so the cycle would continue and my life would go in the same direction as my mother's. But God intervened and didn't allow it to happen because my purpose on this earth carries my destiny. God predestined me for another mission in this life that would require me to be the MOSES of my own family tree. I had to be the one who would deliver my family from what we call in the hood "The Struggle." When God put me in my mother's womb, He put it in me that my purpose would be to lead my family to Him and break a curse that had temporarily claimed my mother. She had no idea what she was carrying and how blessed she really was. Listen up. It can seem like you're carrying something so heavy and stressful right now, but God may very well be giving you the very thing needed to deliver you.

I remember the year I joined the military. I wasn't scared but I remember having a tremendous amount of excitement. That day the recruiter pulled up to my home and everybody on my street was outside. My grandmother was in tears and I can vaguely remember exactly how my mother was reacting to it all, but I do know, looking back, she must have felt a sense of relief and sorrow at the same time, relief that I had made it out of the ghetto and sorrow that she had to stay. That day marked the day the enemy lost a battle and he had to work harder to abort the plan of God on my life. This brings to mind, "if God be for you, who can be against you" (Romans 8:31)?

As I got in the car to head to the airport, my heart was beating fast and I could feel the stares of our neighbors, and I could feel their regret, envy, sadness and love coming at me all at once. I knew I would be on the minds and mouths of my hood for a while because I made a decision that I knew, and the entire block knew, and everyone that saw me get in that government vehicle knew my life had changed. I would never be the same. And I would possibly never come back to the "hood." Boy, were they right about my departure that day.

We must acknowledge that our suffering is necessary to grow. Our mistakes and trauma are just pathways to our purpose. My first marriage was even more tumultuous than my first relationship. The man I married was designed to cultivate me through not loving me and not knowing my value. Some may say, "Wow, that's not good. You shouldn't have had to go through that just to become strong," but on the contrary, I had to go through it to see God's mighty hand, his unwavering love toward me, and his deliverance. Make no mistake about it, God saw it all and knew the whole story because he knew something I wasn't aware of fully. He made me and he knew what he made me out of. He knew what was inside me needed to take this path. God knows what he put into you because He created you, just like Mercedes Benz knows exactly what their vehicles are capable of because they created and built them. Your opinion of someone doesn't affect their potential. The manufacturer, God knows what he made and what that person can do.

There is a saying, "It's just not in them to give." Well, that may be so but could it be they have not tapped into it? Isn't it funny when you break up with someone and the very thing you wanted them to do in the relationship, they somehow manage to give the next person what you always wanted them to give to you? What you think about a person is irrelevant to what a person was created to be.

People have potential but until they walk in it, they haven't walked in their purpose or ability.

My first marriage was based on establishing my identity in God. The devil's job was totally designed to break me and destroy my witness and my anointing. The enemy would use what I call "wearing out tactics" through my ex-husband to try and belittle me and defame me. During that time I knew I had been called to preach the gospel, and he knew as well. I was married for seventeen years and I wanted my marriage to work, but looking back, I recognize you can't expect something from someone who was not created for you to be with.

Even in a marriage you must seek God for the person He created just for you, because God put everything you need inside the person who was created for you. During that season in my first marriage I desperately wanted my ex to appreciate me and support the calling on my life but anything that would seem to prosper me, he would not help me with at all. Sometimes people feel like when you are prospering it's dimming their light. I didn't know this at the time but I had been put in the fire. That marriage would test the very core of me. The enemy wanted me to bow down and curse God but I would often say to myself after crying, "Robin, you must go through this." For some reason God had put something in me that no demon in hell could put out. That was faith. I had faith in knowing he would bring me out. He would give me power over it all one day. Toward the end of my first marriage I knew God was soon gonna deliver me because He would often take me to scriptures of deliverance that would begin to prepare me for separation. God will prepare you for departure. He was showing me that I had served my time and soon he would take the yoke off me.

During that time my only concern was my two sons. I knew my life would soon be different, but I knew I had to make it as smooth as possible for their sake. I have this rare ability that a lot of people don't have and that's being able to place myself in someone else's shoes. I told myself that I would not fight him for total custody because they were his children as well. Many women think that when they leave the relationship the kids should leave as well. I must say that those children deserved their father because it's their right. I decided not to leave Florida so that our youngest son could have his father. By doing that it also gave me freedom to heal from years of crying and emotional abandonment and ultimately the loss of my marriage. I would often see traits of my mother in my ex-husband and now I know that the enemy can wear many masks but one thing is certain, He only has a few tricks. That evil spirit wanted me to feel abandoned and shipwrecked spiritually, then in turn abort the calling on my life, "but God!" Praise break. I can hear the organ playing.

My purpose has been the reason for every event that has taken place in my life. Purpose will find you; purpose will follow you, purpose will knock on your soul day and night until you answer or if you don't answer, it will waste in your grave. Dr. Myles Monroe once said that the richest place on earth is the graveyard. He was so right; so many people died without fulfilling their purpose and giving their ideas to this world. The wealthiest people are the people who have pursued their purposes and allowed themselves to trust the process. This day and age, people think that if they have money, they have fulfilled their purpose. That's a "poor man's mentality." Or if they have lots of things such as houses, cars and land, well, that's a "rich man's mentality." But the person who has ideas, witty inventions and seeks God for their "purpose" is the "wealthy." When you trust that God has your life in the palm of His hand, you become dangerous and a very powerful person on earth because you have all of heaven as your backup and protection. God must honor the purpose he gave you and He must equip you to fulfill it.

The enemy had a plan to silence me from the very moment my mother conceived me. He wanted to make me overwhelmed with abandonment issues early on so that preach the gospel, that open a business, that be a motivational speaker, that minister to the broken-hearted, that overcome a bad marriage and find love again, that overcome rejection, and that I wouldn't be a resilient black woman who is capable of having victory in every area of my life.

My mother has been clean and sober for over seventeen years and she is a faithful believer and successful businesswoman. Through my unwavering obedience, God set her free and delivered her at a church conference in Columbus, Ohio and she has never looked back. My father is married and drug-free as well.

My life is not in vain. I have a marriage that is worth fighting for and an incredible husband who loves me and cherishes me. My tears were bottled up and transformed into a healing river over my life. Hallelujah! The Lord has used me to minister behind and out of the pulpit. Many have been set free because I chose to be a victor and not a victim. The Kingdom of God needs real soldiers who are vulnerable enough to say, "No matter who comes or no matter who goes, I must finish the course set before me. I must see my story as a weapon of warfare to deliver someone from the pit and give them hope for tomorrow."

I used to always ask the Lord, "What's gonna become of me?" I remember having many questions for God about my future, because I really didn't understand the meaning of "purpose." I would be caught up in people and I would often wonder, *Why does this person not like me or why do they have a problem with me?* But boy oh boy, when I understood God's purpose for my life, I welcomed the "smoke," meaning I knew I was somebody with God and whatever fire someone wanted to start, I had enough power in me to put it out; then all that was left was the smoke. Embrace your haters as necessary pieces to your life's purpose. Haters are what you need to develop. I'm not saying welcome them into your home and break bread with them to prove a point, but what I am saying to you is let them talk and spread lies and throw salt on your name. This only puts fuel to flames for your growth and development. They will be witnesses to an amazing triumph like only God knows how to present. He said he will prepare a table before you in the presence of your enemies. So let Him do it.

This may seem crazy but I sometimes think of purpose as a personality trait. I feel that purpose is such a gentleman; it will open doors for you, buy expensive meals, get you in places that you never dreamed you would be invited to, get you tickets to the best events, pay your bills, take care of your children for generations—and all it needs is a willing mind to allow it to work in your life.

Another way I think of purpose is like a seed. Purpose needs good soil to truly be manifested in your life. Your purpose is always waiting to grow.

My life now in my late forties has far exceeded what I thought God would have done for me. He gave me another chance at love with my amazing husband. God has opened the eyes of my understanding in knowing that He has my life in the palm of His hands. Purpose is the key to unlocking God's plan for your life.

Passion is so important when you are trying to figure out what your purpose is. Find the passion and you will see the purpose. I believe in divine order and I believe that everything you encounter in life is in divine order. God doesn't make mistakes. He is the ultimate planner! He will never get you off course when you are seeking out what He has created you to become. There is nothing God won't do for you when you seek Him for all the answers to fulfill His plan for your life. Trust me, He doesn't give you the full picture at once, but I know one thing, He does give you a hopeful end.

Samantha Pierce is the owner of NeuroDiversity Consulting LLC. NeuroDiversity Consulting LLC educates, empowers, and includes, equipping families, individuals, and professionals to create inclusive environments for people with developmental disabilities. She is also the founder of the nonprofit organization Sanchia A. Callender, Inc. The organization's mission is to enrich the lives of people with developmental disabilities and youth in residential care by developing better resources, educating communities, and creating programs to serve their needs.

Samantha utilizes experiences as a wife, mother of autistic people, a woman of faith, and an immigrant woman of color to help educate, include, and empower others, especially those with developmental disabilities. Diagnosis of autism at the age of 43 has deepened her commitment to assisting others in understanding developmental disabilities and making space for those in disabled communities to be included and accepted in the wider community.

Samantha is currently completing an undergraduate degree in psychology and preparing to earn a graduate degree in social work. She is also co-authoring a project about disability and inclusion. In her "spare" time, Samantha spends time with her husband and their five children. Together, they enjoy cooking, gardening, painting, gaming, and arguing over philosophy and current affairs.

FROM SHATTERED SHARDS, SOLACE

Samantha JC Pierce

Shattered

Where do I start this story? August 2017. I crawled into bed for a nice nap on a warm, sunny Sunday afternoon. I received a panicked phone call from one of my sisters before I could fall asleep. One of my sisters had collapsed, and as the closest family member, I needed to rush to her side immediately. I threw some things in an overnight bag, fielding calls from my sister's friends and law enforcement officers on the scene. I filled in my husband and kids on the few details I knew, then I was in the family minivan heading for the highway within fifteen minutes.

I cranked up the radio during the three-hour drive to my sister's city. I imagined joking with my sister about giving the family a scare on a perfect Sunday afternoon. My stomach did weird flips and gurgles throughout the entire drive. A little ember of worry sparked and flickered deep in my mind, trying to get my attention. I pushed it back behind the shutters of my mind, blocking it from conscious view.

I walked into the hospital's emergency department, still rehearsing the jokes I would tell my sister when I made it to her bedside. Her deadpan replies echoed in my mind, making me smile. The hospital staff led me to a waiting room where my sister's friends sat waiting for me. We chatted for a while, waiting for a doctor to come and update us on my sister's status. That little ember of worry in my mind kept trying to get my attention. I kept rehearsing the conversation I would have with my sister when I saw her.

A friendly doctor, who looked not much older than my teenagers, entered the room and pulled up a chair to sit in front of me. I forced myself to make eye contact as he spoke. My sister had collapsed at a church event. Her friends had started CPR immediately and continued until EMTs arrived. The EMTs continued CPR on the back country roads to the hospital. Hospital staff took over the efforts once she arrived. My sister didn't make it despite their efforts.

I felt something inside me break and shatter like a bone forced to bend. That little ember of worry broke free, roared to life, and utterly consumed the conversation I thought I was about to have with my sister. I closed my eyes, shutting out the sight of the concerned faces of the doctor and my sister's friends. I could feel them close around me, lending their comforting presence. I'm sure they said words meant to comfort and console, but I don't know what they were.

So many thoughts flooded my mind at once. It must have been so hard to do CPR on a friend. It must have been hard to wait, whether they knew or didn't know, until I arrived. It must have been so hard for the EMTs and hospital staff to try to save my sister and not succeed. I thought about the conversation that I would not get to have with my sister. I swear I could still hear her voice and her laughter. I thought about the news I would have to share with the rest of the family, my parents, my sisters, my husband, and my children.

Tears flowed, and I became too congested to breathe properly. I switched to problem-solving mode and focused on practical things. I needed decongestants and water. I needed to stop crying and keep breathing. Passing out wasn't an option. I needed to decide who to tell first and how I would say it. Even though I knew it would be a problem later, I ignored the piece inside me that broke when I heard, "She didn't make it."

I don't remember who I called first. Maybe my husband. He calmly accepted the news that life would move forward without my sister. Maybe my two remaining sisters. Their heartrending cries over the phone will never leave me. I called their friends and ensured they had someone to sit with as they grieved. The shattered piece in me splintered a little more each time I repeated, "She's gone."

My sister's pastor came to sit with me and my sister's body while waiting for my parents to arrive. His calm had to be divine, and it was what I needed at the time. I didn't have to worry about him or his feelings, even though part of me thought I should. I paced the empty hospital hallways, wondering how I would tell my parents that their child was gone. How would I want to hear the news that one of my children was dead? I wouldn't. I thought about other families that must be in the hospital somewhere. Were they mourning a missing member? Were they celebrating a recovery? I didn't have any answers.

I checked in on family, and I checked in on friends. I did not check in on myself. I didn't have time to pay attention to that sore, aching place filling with sharp shards inside me. Holding my sister's hands, I thought about death. I would never hear her voice outside of my memory again, I would never see her living smile again, and I could never ask her advice again. But what did death mean for her? Her heart would no longer break over hurting people. She was free from the worries of the living. But how was I supposed to live without her?

My parents finally arrived after more than three hours on the road. The words I had rehearsed deserted me as I led them into the room where my sister's body lay. I watched tears of silent grief well up in my father's eyes while my mother, stubborn as ever, voiced her denial. My sister did not respond to their calls, and my tears flowed fresh.

Shards

The weeks after that deceptively sunny Sunday afternoon were not a blur. The cascade of emotions from those days remains vivid. I pushed my grief and confusion aside and ignored my broken place in favor of helping others grieve—my children, my sisters, my parents. I stayed in my problem-solver mode. What do I do now that my sister is gone? What would her legacy be? I had started work on creating a nonprofit to honor and carry on her work with disabled people and youth in residential care. I was great at distracting myself from my grief.

As the months wore on, I explored the spaces my sister once occupied in my life. I tried to fill the void by getting closer to my remaining sisters, but I couldn't seem to make it work. I kept finding shards of shattered feelings stabbing at my tender places as they tried to heal. My sisters weren't ready to talk about our missing piece with me. They didn't want me to talk about the nonprofit work I was doing in her name. They didn't want to talk to me. I tried to console my parents and my remaining sisters, but the ways that I knew how to help were not what they wanted. I wanted help, but they weren't ready to help me. The shards from the broken place slipped deeper as I longed for their presence and companionship.

I had relied on my dead sister so much that I thought I could depend on the rest of my family in the same way. She was a bridge and shield; I was cut off and exposed once she was gone. My hurt and loneliness turned to anger. Why didn't they want to sit, talk, and be comforted by me? I asked them. I tried my hardest to be honest and communicate how I felt and what I wanted from them. Turns out, they didn't want to give it, and no amount of begging to be loved and accepted in the way that I wanted would make them do as I asked. I was devastated. The people I wanted to be a haven for me were anything but. I'd known this all my life. Growing up, I never really felt comfortable or safe unless I was alone. I realized what had broken inside me. The filters I had kept in place to keep unpleasant truths out and my true feelings in had shattered into millions of glittering shards. They would not go back together. In the months after my sister passed, I realized that as I pulled each of those shards free, I had lobbed them at my sisters, hoping to make them understand my pain. I just wanted to be loved and accepted by the people who helped make me who I am.

The ideal vision that I carried in me of how a family would operate during adversity withered in the face of reality. In my mind, we would come together, hold each other's heads above the water, and swim to safe shores together. Instead, I experienced floundering, drowning, calling for help, and almost losing myself when I realized I was calling on people who couldn't help me. I had a husband and children depending on me. I could not afford to drown waiting for help from people who didn't understand me or know how to help me.

I wasn't sure what to do with myself with my illusions and filters shattered by the loss of my sister. Help people, that's what I would do. That's my default setting. Find a cause and pour myself into it. For years my motivation was to ensure that my autistic children and other children like them got a fair shot at a quality education. That meant being in and out of their classrooms, talking to their teachers, and regularly rolling up at school board meetings.

While I was still figuring out how to adapt to the loss of my sister, I decided to fight for mental health resources for people with developmental disabilities. I added to that by raising awareness about adverse childhood experiences, advocating for trauma-sensitive schools in my city, and teaching people about resilience. All while those shards were digging into my tender broken places.

A little over a month after my sister died, I signed on as a plaintiff in the New Yorkers for Students' Educational Rights lawsuit against New York state. Now I was fighting for equitable funding for public schools in the state. I spent months waiting and preparing, piling on more responsibilities to prove that I was worthy of love and praise from my family. I met with the lawyers representing families in the case. I told them about my five fabulous children and their struggles and triumphs at school. Eventually, I got to testify before an assistant state attorney general. For the first time, during nearly six hours of testimony, I told the story of how one of my developmentally disabled children had been abused by a staff person at school.

But wait, there's more.

"You're right. You're autistic."

Nearly a year before that anticlimactic statement in a doctor's office, a friend asked, "Have you thought you might be autistic? Because everything you tell me about it sounds like you too."

"Funny you asked that, friend." Months of trying and failing to connect with my sisters helped me realize that other human beings made no sense to me, except maybe for the ones I was raising myself. Some days I wasn't sure I had them figured out either. No matter how much data I collected on their behaviors or how many notes I took on what they said, there always came the point that people were just baffling.

I don't know if you know this but getting an autism diagnosis is difficult. You wait as long as twelve to eighteen months to get an appointment with someone who will talk to you about the testing options. Then you wait some more months for the appointments where the actual testing happens. I had been raising my autistic children for nearly twenty years. My eldest autistic child had once declared, "Mom, you're just like me!" "Yes, son. I sort of did notice." I had seen his teenage brain problem-solve as I did as a teenager. But it took the shattering of my shield and filters after my sister died for me to start suspecting the truth. As I was piling more and more responsibilities on myself, I was also coming to terms with the fact that I had been autistic all along. A lot of my life started to make sense – the preference for quiet, and books and the curiosity and rapid-fire questions that always zipped through my brain; the ease with which I understood some things and the struggles I had making sense of others.

Solace

Guess what happens next in my story? Go on, guess. If I'm doing this right, it should be clear where this story is going. You got it – burnout. I was so mad at myself when I finally realized what had happened. This wasn't the first time I had found myself in a pit of despair. I had clawed my way out once after learning that the pit was not where God wanted me to live. What was I doing back in it, just as deep as before? I wasn't supposed to make that mistake again. At the time, I voiced my complaints to my therapist.

"But you know how to get back out of the pit, right? You know you can do the work because you've done it before. And you were good at it."

"Well, yeah. But I didn't like this pit the first time I was here," I whined.

Resilience is not a one-and-done. I wish it was. It is a process that lasts a lifetime. The hurt that can be done in a few seconds with a few words can take a lifetime to heal. "You ain't no use!" I heard that a lot growing up. I was told that I couldn't get anything right, as bright as I was. My timing was always off. Too much time reading, too much time doing chores, too much time outside, too much time inside. I'm not sure there was anything that I ever got right.

Resilience is getting back up when the bullies beat you down. It is believing in yourself in the face of critics. It is maintaining your curiosity even when people tell you that you ask too many questions. The day in junior high school that I pinned a bully to the lockers so he couldn't land any blows on me was when the bullies stopped coming for me. It was a day that I could have realized my strength, but I was still young and didn't know who I really was.

Resilience is caring for the emotional wounds I receive so they don't fester and spread infection. I care for my scars so they remain soft, supple, and flexible instead of stiff, unbending, and always in pain. I've learned to take care of the broken place filled with the shards of my old shields and filters. I'm gentle with myself as I remove each one, examine it, and set it aside. I remind myself that even if I get hurt, healing and recovery are possible. Not easy, but possible.

There are no easy fixes. Some problems don't have solutions on this side of eternity. So what do I do? I endure. I've learned to cast my cares on God. I'm not talking about leaving a neatly wrapped package at the foot of the cross. I stumble forward in the dark, collapse in fear and frustration, and cut loose like a tired, hangry toddler. God knows how to comfort me no matter how much I act up or how miserable I am. The Lord is my refuge when I can't deal with myself or the rest of humanity. He knows how to feed me and give me rest. He knows how to restore me to balance when I become dysregulated. I can trust him to do it all without scolding me for struggling with the burdens that are too great for me to carry alone.

"God, this is so heavy. It's too heavy for me."

"You're right, daughter. Let me help you."

"Gratitude makes sense of our past, brings peace for today, and creates a vision for tomorrow."

Melody Beattie

Denika Lundy was born and raised in Syracuse, New York. She is the co-founder of 2Sisters4Life Breast cancer awareness. Her story starts way before she was thought of. A long lineage of breast and ovarian cancer has stricken her family. Denika shares her early thoughts and experiences and how she's had to fight through her own journey and battle with breast cancer.

Denika has traveled and spoken to the masses from New York to Gabon, Africa. She will continue to tell her story in hopes of increasing knowledge and a higher survival rate. Denika is a 20-year breast cancer SURVIVOR! After reading her story your faith will be stronger. You will notice and count your blessings; you will rise and be counted!

MOM SAID, "RISE AND BE COUNTED!"

Denika Lundy

I have seen it, over and over: breast cancer in my family. It just kept coming back. I was young, maybe eight or nine, when I saw my Aunt Cindy bald. She always had a blanket covering her. There were times I saw her with a wig on and then there were times she had her own dark hair. My Aunt Cindy was a mother and wife; she was an artist and fought to stay alive to watch her son graduate. And she did. She took her rest after battling breast cancer for seventeen years. She was forty-seven. My Aunt Cindy stood up and was counted!

My mother was forty-two when she found out that she had cancer. The first time I saw her in the hospital after her surgery, I walked in her room and I looked at her, and I couldn't control my emotions. I told her, "I can't." I ran away crying. It hit me like a ton of bricks, the thought that I might lose my mother. She didn't lose her hair, so it wasn't as visual as Aunt Cindy that she had cancer. She was happy to get her implants. My mother had tiny breasts all her life and didn't care that the implants were rock hard. She was light about the subject of cancer. She didn't tell me much, but I was a teenager and possibly didn't ask. One thing that comes to mind at least once a week is a memory of my mom. She was in the shower, and she called my name. "Nika." I went into the bathroom and she asked me to shave her underarms. My eyebrows rose. "Huh?" She said, "I can't feel anything under my arms and I don't want to cut myself." A blanket of emotions took over and I realized I had to step up and take care of my mom. When she took a shower, I stayed close to hear my name and to take care. My mother taught me how to love; she made us feel important. She would take me and my sister Dory to a small corner deli to get fresh turkey sandwiches, yogurt, and a cookie before school most mornings because Dory didn't like school lunch. My mother knew us. She tried to make us feel special the best way she could in those times. She passed away in 1994. She was forty-five. My mother Robin stood up and was counted!

I was twenty-seven when I was diagnosed with invasive breast cancer. I was a young wife and mother of two boys: Damian, four years old, and Dimitrius, fifteen months. I felt the lump. It was under my arm going toward my breast. I started losing weight. I had bruises on my hip bones from hitting the sink when I did dishes. I waited six months to see a doctor. My Aunt Susan, my mother's youngest sister, felt my lump and said, "I don't like it, Nika. It's hard, it doesn't move." She urged me to go to the doctors, so I did.

My primary care doctor was visibly nervous after doing my exam. After I told him my family's history with breast cancer, he sent me to get a mammogram and nothing showed up. At twenty-seven, I had dense breasts, which is typical for young women. Next, I was sent to get an ultrasound and it showed my tumor, so I was referred for a biopsy, all within three days. I had many doctor appointments. My husband and younger son, who I was still breastfeeding, came with me.

The office seemed busy. We waited for over an hour. My one-year-old was getting tired. I went back in and told them I would come back another day. She asked my name and as soon as it came off my lips, everyone stopped to help me. They said, "No, please come this way. We will bring your family to you." I was led to the doctor's actual office, my family entered, and we sat less than one minute before he entered the room. He sat at his desk and came right out and said, "Denika, you have breast cancer." My husband took a deep breath, eyes wide open, looking at me and our son.

I asked, "Am I going to die?"

"Not if I can help it!" my doctor said. "We will start with getting you a port for chemotherapy because we don't want your veins to dry out. It's very aggressive and we need to shrink it."

Everything sounded like blah-blah-blah.

Things moved quickly; it wasn't until my first appointment that I realized. I was led into a room and sat down. The nurse gave me a gown and asked me to have it open in the front. She said the doctor would be in soon and sat a folder down and walked out the door. I changed. The air was cool and it gave me a chill. I noticed the folder and I opened it.

Twenty-seven-year-old female. Stage two breast cancer. I stopped reading because I felt like I was snooping. The doctor came in and picked up the folder, looked at me and said, "Denika?" I looked up and said, "Yes?"

"I see you have a history in your family of breast cancer." *Wait, that's my folder she's reading. I have breast cancer.*

Within two weeks my mother-in-law treated me to a haircut for chemo. It was to help prepare me for the shock. I have had long hair all my life. My husband was with me for my first treatment. They poked me in the port and the medicine went right to my bloodstream. It burned my nose and gave me a headache and my eyes watered. After a while, either I got used to it or the side effects lessened. Treatment lasted three hours. As soon as I got home my body treated me like the enemy. I violently threw up every twenty minutes for five straight days. I was so weak I couldn't hold anything down. My husband was having trouble with all this. He was annoyed with me. I was in bed. I had gallons of vomit that needed to be cleaned up. I got thin and I looked dry. I could not do anything but lie in bed. He worked and had to come home to me. I couldn't cook or clean or take care of myself. I was useless. We didn't have a connection anymore. But I saw a glimpse of his kindness toward me. It was one of the times he was going through the motions asking me if I was hungry. I couldn't think straight because I was so sick so I wouldn't get anything. I was crying when he came in and he walked toward me, and asked me, "What's wrong?" I said, "I stink and it smells in here and I need help to get clean." He bathed me. He was gentle and he seemed sad, like he wanted to do better. I knew he wouldn't. And when I felt like I was a burden to ask to get bathed, maybe that was on my mind. We were both so young, and neither of us was prepared for all the interruptions of life.

The second week after chemo, I was very sleepy. I couldn't lift my head up off the pillow. By the third week I had some energy and motivation to get up. Well, I got up, but a chunk of my hair stayed on the pillow. I asked my husband to shave it off. It was real; now I looked as sick as I was.

At the end of the third week, it was time to do it all over again. By now I was bald. We were struggling at the time, living with his grandmother with our two little boys. Our relationship had just been through something and this diagnosis came as soon as we made amends. We were not strong enough.

Sometimes God puts people in your life strategically. A package arrived. It was from the twins, two girls I grew up with since middle school, Teresa and Falisha. Teresa knew I lost weight, so she sent me panties that fit. They sent soft night clothes, snacks for the boys and the best gifts of all were a Bible and Yolanda Adams'

CD. I played the CD on repeat. I sang it. I yelled it. I cried the words to "That Name Jesus." My mind started to get stronger.

Here we go again, round two: By this time my husband left to go work in another city for two to three months while his wife had chemotherapy, a four-year-old and a one and a half-year old to take care of. "That name Jesus"—I didn't know that I was beginning to rise and be counted!

My brother-in-law stepped up and drove me to chemo. I was a little embarrassed. I wasn't sure if he was just dropping me off or staying. He parked and escorted me to the office. He said he would be right here when I was done. Silently, I was screaming on the inside, "Rene, please come sit with me," but it didn't come out. Instead, I said, "Ok, see you in a few hours." My brother-in-law was there on time. On the way home he took me to lunch at Red Lobster. It would have been exactly what I wanted any other time, but as soon as the food came, we had them bag it up. During our drive home, he had to stop three times for me to throw up. He was kind to me, and patient.

By the third week I felt stronger. Rene called me and said a friend of his was going to bring me some food from Wendy's. It couldn't have been better timing because I was hungry and my kids were asleep. I heard a car pull up. I got up quickly, not wanting to make his friend wait. I opened the door and this pretty green-eyed, caramel-complexioned girl with fat Jamaican braids walked up and with the softest voice said, "You're the prettiest bald lady I ever saw."

I said, "Thank you." But I didn't believe it.

She asked me if she could come in and eat with me. I said, "Yes, please." I had been craving conversation. Nytima had two daughters the same ages as my boys. She stuck around and we developed a true friendship.

I gave my son Dimitrius a party for his second birthday. Some people seemed uncomfortable with my bald head. I lived in Miami and it was hot so I couldn't please everyone. My husband was still away.

Round three: My mother-in-law drove me. She talked about praying and keeping the faith. She dropped me off and told me Rene would pick me up. He did and dropped me off. This one was bad. Again, every twenty minutes for five days straight, I vomited. One night my son Damian, who was four years old at the time, said, "Mom, we have to call 911. I think you're going to die; it's too much." That name Jesus! We got through that night and the nights that came. I went through a tiring week and then had strength again.

Round four: red lipstick, bald and no eyelashes. I drove myself, but I didn't tell them that. I sashayed into the office, was greeted with smiles, and I gave an amazing light. They did the normal blood work to see my red and white blood cell count. I had about an hour to go when they stopped the treatment and asked me how I was feeling. It turned out my blood count was very low. They could not believe I was walking, let alone smiling. They stopped my chemo. They said they needed to figure this out because the treatment was killing me slowly. At this point I just went with the flow. No more treatment. I drove home after only half a treatment. *Why am I so sick?*

My husband was back home and it was my worst week, non-stop vomiting. My husband checked on me throughout the day. He started in the morning and came back twice for lunch and dinner. "Are you hungry?" Each time I paused too long or couldn't think of what to eat since I couldn't hold anything down. Every time, he'd say, "Let me know if you want something" and leave. I would just go back to sleep. Finally in the evening when he came in, I would ask for water.

The next morning, he took the boys to his mother's house. Yadira, my first friend that I made in Florida, stopped over. She gasped when she saw me and said, "I'll be back." Within thirty minutes she was back. She had a jug of water, Dole peaches, tea bags, and cleaning supplies. She dumped my pail; she bathed me; she changed my sheets; and she mopped the floor. She did all this without making me feel less than. She put lotion on my head. She sat and talked with me and cared for me. I count my blessings. Yadira rose up and is surely counted!

Time passed and I was getting stronger. I started looking healthy. My body was smaller but cute; my hair was growing and it looked like a sassy cut. One day my friend, Maricarmen, brought me bags of clothes that she had purchased for me. She told me she just wanted me to feel good and look good. Wow, I just kept receiving. God is so good to have these people in my life. Teresa, Falisha, Rene, Julianna, Nytima, Yadira, and Maricarmen—you all rose up and have been counted!

A year after I had healed from my surgeries—a port put in for chemotherapy; a double mastectomy and tram flap (which takes the fat from my belly and transfers it to my breast); two additional surgeries for my port because it got infected; and a full hysterectomy at thirty years old (if I did not get the hysterectomy, it was very likely I would be dead by thirty-two because there is a direct link from breast cancer to ovarian cancer)—I got a phone call from my sister Dory. She said, "Nika, I have a lump in my breast." She was twenty-seven. My heart broke for my little sister, who is eighteen months younger than me.

There was a lot going on at the time. My marriage was failing. My kids and I moved back to Syracuse, where I'm from. Dory started chemo. When we arrived in Syracuse, Dory was in her third week of treatment. I was able to clean and cook and take care of her. I was able to help and be there for my niece, Ataliya, who was nine years old. I couldn't believe that my sister was in the same place I was one year before. I walked in her room and said, "Okay Sis, let's get in the shower." She lifted her head from the pillow and said, "I don't think I can, Nika." I knew that feeling and was saddened that now she knew it too. I gently told her, "I got you, sissy." I did everything I could to help and to uplift her dignity. I got in the shower with her with no extra thoughts, other than to make her feel better. She did it. She was a survivor.

Eight years later, I got a call while at work. "Denika, you have a call on line one." I knew it was Dory because it was close to lunch time and that's when we met every day.

"Hellloooo Darling." She was crying. A cry that was so sad to hear my eyes teared up.

"What's wrong, Sis?"

"Nika, I feel a lump. It's big, it doesn't move, and it's hard."

My sister was diagnosed with stage four metastatic breast cancer and it was in her bones. She had tumors in her knee, pelvis, and neck. Chemotherapy was no longer an option. No surgery could fix it. She received some radiation to stabilize it.

I asked the doctor, "What do we do now?" Her answer was that we should travel the world. That was not our reality. I owned a house and a vehicle but lived paycheck to paycheck.

The night before Dory's last radiation treatment, my house caught on fire. There was a lot of damage and we were displaced for over a year. I started to receive checks from the insurance company while my house was getting rebuilt. I took the doctor's advice. We visited New York City, North Carolina, Florida, Las Vegas, Jamaica and celebrated Dory's thirty-fifth birthday in Mexico. Our conversations changed. We started writing down plans to help give our inner-city community breast health knowledge, because knowledge is power. While in New York City we got tattoos. My tattoo was on the left, representing her cancer and hers was on the right, representing mine: 2Sisters4Life. It was to remind us that we need to tell our story, get the conversation going in hopes of a better survival rate in inner-city communities. My sister Dory said she got cancer twice because she took it from her daughter. My niece Ataliya does not have the gene. Dory took her final rest on July 9, 2011, forever 35.

My beautiful sister, I will continue to say your name every day and I will gladly fill your shoes as a grandmother to SkyeMarie. I kept our focus and continued with our plans to have conversations about breast cancer awareness. Since 2013 I have spoken in schools and churches. I've done trainings with women's groups. I've been interviewed on radio and TV stations from New York to Jamaica. I went to Gabon, Africa and spoke to one hundred fifty people. I told my story. I expressed my concerns for young people thinking that cancer is an older person's disease; it is not. Cancer does not discriminate and men are not exempt.

We thought cancer was over for my family, but it reared its ugly head again. My older sister Aimee had a pain in her back that she shared with her doctors. Nothing happened for a while, until she kept discussing her concern and then she was diagnosed with stage three ovarian cancer. She was fifty years old when she received her diagnosis. Our nanny, grandmother, had ovarian cancer and passed away one year later. That is not Aimee's story. She is now a four-year ovarian cancer survivor. My sister worked the entire time, throughout her treatments. She is a powerhouse. She continues to rise and be counted!

One thing most people don't know is, as a cancer survivor, I must continue to think good thoughts. It's way too easy to lay down and die, to give up or give in to the negative. We have had body parts taken from us; we have had to cut food supply from our infants. Our relationships are tested. We wear our scars daily, even if they are covered. They make a huge impact on our lives forever. Even with faith a fear comes up at each checkup. We feel alone in a crowded room. Lord, please heal us from the inside out. This is my life and I want it. I want to yell from the rooftop, CHANGE YOUR

WAY OF THINKING. At a young age we start being ugly to each other and that creates stress and stress can lead to cancer. Teach our children kindness. Be kind to each other. Let's all rise and be counted!

"There are two primary choices in life: to accept conditions as they exist or accept the responsibility for changing them."

Denis Waitley

Yolanda Clemons-Brown is a licensed Family Nurse Practitioner. She has been a nurse for over 25 years working in many nursing capacities including ER nursing, geriatrics, corrections, education, and diabetes.

Yolanda is a native of New York City. She graduated from LaGuardia High School of Music & Performing Arts in Manhattan, majoring in vocal music. She moved to Syracuse, NY in the late 80's where she obtained her bachelor's and master's degree in nursing and met her husband of 25.5 years while attending college.

Yolanda is a worshiper at heart and knows she was "chosen" to worship God. She assisted in leading worship at her church, Abundant life Christian Center for over 10 years.

In 2021, Yolanda became a widower, losing her husband to ALS. Her goal is to be a walking testimony to those who have experienced loss, trials and tribulations. Through her transparency and realness, she hopes to give insight and truth concerning the matters of the heart. She continues her healing journey, which is a lifetime process.

Yolanda has two sons, three daughters, and two grandsons. She currently resides in McDonough, GA with her two youngest children. She loves music and spending quality time with her loved ones.

LESSONS FROM LOU

Yolanda C. Brown

My name is Yolanda C. Brown, I am a mother of five and a grandmother of two. I am a believer who loves to worship. I am a woman who has had and who has lost. I am a spiritual woman living a human experience. I am a nurse by trade, and I am a widow.

In 2017 the love of my life was diagnosed with ALS - Amyotrophic Lateral Sclerosis. ALS is a progressive nervous system disease that affects nerve cells in the brain and spinal cord, causing loss of muscle control and eventually death. ALS is also called Lou Gehrig's disease. This disease was named after the baseball player Lou Gehrig, who was diagnosed June 19, 1939. To this day doctors and scientist are not sure how and or why ALS develops in the body. They are not clear as to why some get it and why others do not. Unfortunately, my husband of 25.5 years passed away April 21, 2021. He fought for four long years. We endured and watched as this disease took over his body, yet never did it touch his smile or tenacity to live.

I decided to name this chapter Lessons from Lou for obvious reasons. So many lessons were learned during this time frame. I have a saying: Life continues to offer us lessons and blessings. If you learn from a lesson then truly it is a blessing. I've learned so much about myself that it blew my mind. The relationship between me and God unexplainably grew and continues to grow to this day. I miss my husband so very much. This void is heavy. I wouldn't wish this pain on anyone, not even my worst enemy. It is at times overwhelming and unbearable. I decided to share some of these learned lessons with you, with the hopes that you will appreciate and learn from them as well.

She's a runner!

After my husband's death, I felt empty and incomplete. Yes, I had Christ, I had Jehovah, the great I Am, and I knew God was my provider, my comforter, and my protector. I also knew he was going to get me through this. I continued to worship at church and praise God from the platform. I sang my troubles away until even that was no longer dulling the ache. You see, I not only lost my husband to ALS in April of 2021, I also lost two sisters to COVID-19. My second eldest sister passed away in October of 2020 and my eldest sister passed away in March of 2021. I had three major losses all within six months. The memory of it all makes my heart palpate and my spirit grieve.

I was angry with GOD. I couldn't understand why. I was so filled with anger, grief, unforgiveness, confusion, and sexual frustration—yes, I said it. I was filled with all of this and possibly more. I wanted a way out and I wanted one real fast. Therefore, I ran. I ran from state to state and sought the attention of men who were less than deserving.

When one finds oneself infected with all these negative emotions and attributes, one's alignment with the Father is off. When that alignment is off your focus becomes distorted. My perspective on life was cloudy, to say the least. I had decided to do it all my way. I constantly ran from the pain and myself. I didn't know this new self and deep down, I didn't want to get to know this new me. All I knew was sitting still hurt way too much. When I was still, I had to reflect on the pain and my reality. The reality of feeling and being alone, middle-aged, an empty nester and afraid was more than overwhelming. I would tell myself I was a new slate, new wine skin, new tapestry, and in all actuality, I was a new hot mess. I was a 49- to 50-year-old woman with the mind frame of a 17- to 18-year-old fool. I carelessly spent money I should have invested. I became prey to many vultures, knowing this all could have been avoided if I had just sat still and listened to the voice of God.

The Vultures and the lesson

Life has a funny way of teaching us valuable lessons. Lessons that hurt are needed. Many may be familiar with the saying, "Be careful of what you ask (pray) for because you just might get it." In this season, I have prayed and continued to pray for wisdom and direction. I asked God to open my eyes to the things unseen and hidden from me. He has done this very thing, and I'm sure he will continue to honor my prayer request, as he has done so many times before.

What's the point of all of this? Well, God revealed three things to me. He showed me the wolf, the leech, and the hater. I'm sure you all know what's coming.

I have had people in my life who appeared to be sheep, but they were really wolves in sheep's clothing, trying to portray Godly values but presenting with devious and childish ways. I have come across so-called friends who sucked the very life from me. Repeatedly, I allowed myself to be used for their selfish gains. They attached themselves to me like leeches, draining what was placed inside of me by God himself. The last group were the haters. These individuals befriended me just so they could sit back and watch for my demise. They don't understand why some can have joy and peace even during a horrible storm. They may even claim to know God, yet they can't understand why and how one can continue to smile. Sadly, it angers them and causes them to react in ways that are shameful and hurtful.

Stay with me, now; this is not said to talk about old friends because I am bitter, angry, disappointed, or filled with regrets. This is mentioned because in this, God showed me myself. He revealed to me who I was, who I am now, and the woman I will one day become.

I had to ask myself, "Why couldn't you see who these people were? What was it about them that attracted you to them?" Then God said, "You were blinded by insecurities, defeat, depression, weakness, and most importantly, lack of joy. My joy." Long story short, we are the company we keep. I was the company I kept. I was all of them rolled up in one. I didn't see them coming because I was comfortable with the me in them.

I am grateful, gratefully broken! God had to empty me out so that he could fill me up. He filled me with his joy, his peace, and his presence in this season. I have been stripped of people and things that did not and will not line up with my destiny and his purpose for me and my life. I realized everything I'm going through is for my good and my benefit. Therefore, I have no regrets. I have some apologies to make. I openly apologize to the wonderful people in my life that I took for granted. I assumed they would always be there, taking for granted how genuine their love for me was and is. I assumed their thoughts and their opinions were not relevant—how wrong I was. I had to ask for forgiveness. God has given me new eyes to see. My sight continues to grow clearer in this season of change. I have and still experience a sense of supernatural peace and calmness. This is how I know God has me and continues to walk with me. Thank you, Father, for the continued life lessons.

Then He spoke!

I smiled but I hurt. I trusted God, yet I was still filled with hurt. The kids left the nest, and I was left with me. Since I can remember, I have had to take care of someone else. As a young child I took care of my baby sister, nieces and nephews. I left home at seventeen and took care of college friends, met my husband fell in love and took care of him and then our children. I even became a nurse so I could take care of others. I joined the church and the choir, where I was able to take care of the body of Christ in and through worship. I say all of this to say that I have taken care of so many and never knew how to truly take care of myself.

In this new season I was given a clean slate. I was given the opportunity to start anew. I made some mistakes; none of us are perfect. I decided to smile and believe that better days are coming. I don't know what tomorrow will bring but I know who holds my future. This is how I continue to encourage me.

I found myself crying out to God during this time. Funny thing is, I didn't cry out for help; I cried out with anger and frustration in my heart. I have been angry with him and mad at my situation. I said, "God I was a good wife, a good mother, a good sister, and a good friend. I followed your word. I crossed my T's and dotted my I's." I said, "Father, I am angry and mad at you for allowing me to be here alone and out here by myself. My husband is gone, my sisters are gone, some of the children have left and some of my amazing friends are gone."

That's when it happened. I heard a small voice whisper gently in my ear. He said, "It's OK; you can be mad at me." He said, "It doesn't matter what you did wrong or right; all that matters is that I got you even in this!" I cried some more, and a calm came over me like never before. You see, God loves us even in our worst hour. He loves us through the heartaches and pain. He loves us in spite of us.

If all our I's and T's are dotted and crossed, that means our race is finished. I was reminded by God that my race is far from finished. It is only the beginning.

Once I recognized his voice, I decided to have a love affair with myself. I decided to smile even when I didn't feel like it. I decided to wear pretty clothes and good smelling oils and lotions daily. I decided to wake up every morning and say, "Hey queen, you are not alone." I made it a point to tell myself how beautiful I am inside and out. I began to embrace the extra skin under my arms, the stretch marks and rolls on my stomach. I embraced the cellulite on both legs. I began to look in the mirror daily and say, "I love you and I'm here for you!" I continue working on becoming selfless and I will continue to love me. I'm already loved and chosen for a season such as this. It was in this season I learned that I was the daughter of the most-high God, who loves me unconditionally.

Lesson of love, loss and brokenness

We sometimes face many losses. In life, we lose jobs, businesses, relationships, family members, etcetera. My God, these things no longer exist! Experiencing the death of what we have in mind or can remember can be heavy. One can say, "I'm accustomed to change," yet are we? Are we truly ready to face the end of what we call normal? I must be honest; I wasn't and at times I continued to struggle with it. I was so gently reminded, "when God restores your life you have to be willing to give up what you remember and change what you call normal." ~ TD Jakes

I was asked, can you have less and serve God? I said yes, I encourage you as I was encouraged. Don't cry about what is in the past, and what is lost, let's thank the creator for what is left.

Things don't always turn out the way you planned, or the way you think they should be. I've learned that there are things that go wrong and aren't always easily fixed or put back together the way they were before. I've learned that some broken things stay broken; yet and still, one can get through bad times while looking for better ones to come.

Staying Focused!

I decided to share this thought with you all. I remembered talking to a dear friend about why people leave the church. People leave for so many reasons. We can talk about them all day long, but instead I will talk about me and pray that it helps someone else. A few years ago, I found myself in a state of isolation, in the ICU of God. I was angry, bitter and confused, to say the least. I wouldn't be able to handle what I am dealing with today if I had not gone through that storm and come out strong. I was not released from my local church, and I praise God that I listen to his voice and not my emotions or feelings. So I sat down. Lesson learned: As a mid-level medical provider in the natural, God speaks to me and meets me in this very environment from time to time. After the loss of my family members and my husband, I was broken. I was infected with jealousy, anger, betrayal, bitterness, and gossip, to name a few. To me, I was wounded in the worst way. I mentioned this because when we go through certain things in life, we look to our church leaders to help us and sometimes support us. When that doesn't happen, we become angry and bitter and sometimes we walk away when we really shouldn't. This is the time we should stand firm and seek God, not man, like never before. While talking to a dear friend it came to me so plainly. When we need our yearly check-ups or need help with common illnesses, we see our primary care physician. Our primary care physician sees hundreds of patients yearly. They take care of many. Yet when we are seriously ill, we see a specialist. A good primary care provider will send you to a specialist, knowing that management of a particular illness may or may not be within his or her scope of practice.

I was reminded by God of my very own spiritual ICU moment. I was not taken care of by the leaders in the church. They provided me with a prescription and a referral called the word of God and prayer, but the head physician, God, took care of me in the ICU with a team of specialists, some I knew in passing and some I didn't know at all. They were not the regular physicians and nurses I was used to seeing in the clinic called church. I was being taken care of by individuals chosen by God to take care of the illnesses that affected me and hindered me from developing and walking in true relationship with him. Remember, primary care providers do not visit ICUs. So please don't look for leaders, especially good leaders, to visit you there either. Only God will decide who takes care of you in those moments. Remember our church leaders-primary care physician sees hundreds, sometimes thousands, in a year. God loves us so much that he will assign specialists to us when we need them most because God sees us. I SEE YOU is what God wants you to know. He wants us to know he loves us, and he wants a relationship with us. In the ICU is where that relationship is often developed.

It is my relationship with God that keeps me today and forever more. I realize that I am no longer used by God, but I walk in relationship with God, and that is the difference. Family, don't walk away from a spiritually fed church (clinic) because you are sick. Check yourself and seek counsel from your leaders, your primary care physician. If he or she sends you off with a prescription or referral for prayer and the word of God, know that they are sending you to the Father, the chief physician. He will admit you in his intensive care unit and there a team of specialists he has chosen will help you heal. But you must be willing. We never want to leave the ICU of God against medical advice (A.M.A.), against the will of God concerning our life. It is a hard place to be but remember what the enemy uses for harm, the God we serve will use that moment of isolation and illness for his glory and our benefit.

The great physician

The loss of our dear loved ones can hit hard, to say the least. The scars I have run deep; boldly I can say they may never go away.

Yes, I'm grateful. These wounds, these scars that run deep didn't leave me infected. I wasn't left infected with unforgiveness, doubt, depression, and despair. My wounds no longer leak with the stench of confusion, revenge, anger, self-doubt and fear.

I have an amazing physician and he is skilled at assessing, diagnosing, treating, and suturing. He assessed my situation, diagnosed my pain, treated the signs and symptoms associated with my loss and sutured my wounds. This great physician's name is Jehovah, Yahweh. Through the sacrifice of Christ, I was afforded top-notch antibiotics called love, patience, correction, hope, redemption, and most importantly, forgiveness. Once the infection was cleared, the master, the great physician, was able to carefully and gracefully put me back together. These scars will forever remain. Yet his sutures left no scars for the naked eye to see. I still cry from time to time. My scars even itch with fury, causing me to remember what cut deep. Then, I'm reminded I hear his voice sweetly say, "I will never leave you nor forsake you." I'm so glad I don't look like what I've been through. This great physician is available to us all. His office is always open, and there's no waiting list or unavailable spot in his schedule. He lives within us all. Why don't you give him a call? Set up an appointment. I promise you won't ever regret the greatest visit and coded healing!

Concerning death concerning life

Continue to hold on with everything you have. It may seem like a horrible nightmare, because it is. It may even seem like you will never wake up from it. Some days that feeling is so real that it causes you to even be mad at God. I assure you it's OK; he's big enough to handle it. Time doesn't heal anything. I'm here to tell you the truth. We just learn how to cope as time goes on. Some days are better than others. Some moments are better than others. I don't know why terrible things in life happen to us or our families. I do know that we have everything we need to get through it. You have love all around you; grab hold of it like your life depends on it. Believe me when I say it does. Love will get you through it. This journey forward won't be easy. Mistakes will be made. Painful words will be spoken, and pain will consume you like never before. But whatever you do, don't judge you. We are not perfect. Just humans trying to live in pain we at times don't understand. Do your best every day. Don't try to overdo or under-do. Just do your best in whatever situation you are in or whatever circumstance has been given. Just do your best. I say again, hold on and hold tight to the love around you and within you. If you look deep and hard, it's there—I promise. On purpose smile, even when you don't feel like it. On purpose get up and thank God for the healing now. On purpose thank him for the blessings that are to come, because they are coming. On purpose hold tight to that mustard seed faith; in times like this that's all we have—hell, that's all we can probably obtain. No one said this journey was going to be easy. I'm here to tell you that it is not. So each day we can decide to walk forward; each day we can decide to get up and go. This day we can decide to live and, most importantly, love.

Journey

Journeys and new beginnings aren't always easy. Still if you choose to journey and begin again with the father, the trip will truly be worth your while.

Feeling like you have no access

I had a dream that I went into a store house with a dear friend. I didn't have access to the supplies. I didn't have a ticket. The funny thing was I was able to go inside and look but I couldn't get anything on my own. My dear friend had access; she had a ticket. She looked at me and said, "Tell me what you want, and I will get it for you." As soon as I awoke God spoke to me.

He said, "Daughter, continue to trust me and like your friend, I will bless you even when you do not have access. You will see, when man says no, trust me, for I will become your access. Wait on me and I will supply all your needs." God continues to grant us access. Let's just wait on him.

Thank you, Lou, for the lessons learned. Even though I have lost a great deal, I am so grateful for the lessons and wisdom obtained. What a great and powerful gift.

Melinda Denice Agnew was born and raised in Syracuse, NY. She is a mother to three children, and the caregiver of her elderly mother. She is a Program Manager of Day Habilitation through Arc of Onondaga Non-Profit Agency. Melinda holds an Associate degree in Human Service Social Work. She acquired a bachelor's degree in Community and Human Services. She anticipates obtaining her master's degree in December of 2022, in Social and Public Policy and a Certificate in Child and Family Services.

Melinda worked in public schools for seven years and she is an advocate for Community Center of Alternatives in Syracuse, NY. When she is not working or cultivating herself, she loves to bond with her family and work on her personal relationship with God.

ANGER
A Normal Human Emotion That You Can Overcome

Melinda Agnew

"Remember, the moment you accept total responsibility for everything in your life is the moment you claim the power to change anything in your life." -Hal Elrod, *The Miracle Morning*

What is anger, and why are so many individuals exhibiting resentment toward themselves and others? I can identify very well with all of them because of my own anger issues. I held a dangerous anger problem that could have left me with serious consequences. My temper started at an early age. It was around the time that my mother and father had separated. I was maybe seven or eight years old. I know I was in the first grade when my mother moved away from my dad.

I felt socially awkward growing up here in Syracuse, New York. I was tall and big for my age, making me stand out as a girl. People used to mistake me for a boy, and I felt offended. I was not the average size like other young girls, not to mention I wore a Jheri curl most of my young life, until I turned sixteen, when my dad let me go to the hairdresser on my own. I was torn between both of my parents because I loved them both equally and felt caught in the middle of their separation. My family used to consist of three sisters from my mother's side, as well as two sisters, two brothers, and my god-brother (who was raised with us) on my dad's side. Before my parents split, we all used to be under one roof. We lived on the Hill, or Hill Top East and West, but it was considered the East Side. I was the baby of the bunch, and I was spoiled rotten. Yet my world was shaken by the age of seven. My mom moved to Kennedy Square apartments on the East Side and in the hood. The loss that I felt from the split of my family was devastating. And over time, I became angrier, then cold wrath lay dormant within me. So in the first grade, I had become the class clown, and I was a fighter. I would do my work and then clown around with my friends.

The kids my age really did not bother me. I had learned how to crack jokes, and I would clown people all day. I was fun to be around, and one thing about me is, I love to laugh. Yet I walked around with a deadly rage lurking inside me. One day in first grade, my teacher became upset with me and some other students. We were cracking jokes with the kids in the back of the room. She thought that our work was not done, but it was. We were interrupting her class. So she told us that we had lunch detention. I told her that I was not going to eat lunch. She replied that I had to go and eat lunch.

Well, when she moved my desk and tried to force me to leave the classroom, I then slapped her glasses off her face. I did not want to go to the lunchroom, and my anger started manifesting when she tried forcing me. The fourth and fifth graders used to pick on me because of my height and weight. They teased me all day during school. I used to hear, "Do you want to see the big first grader?" They spoke quietly and snickered because they knew I would fight them. I was put out of school for fourteen days. During that time, Syracuse City School District just had implemented an in-school suspension. This was the era when you received a paddling for misconduct. I received my consequences at the hearing.

I stood out from the average students. Being a tall and solid girl used to be a challenge for me. What others do not understand about me is that I may look mean but no, I am assertive, and I am a sensitive person. I speak respectfully about what is on my mind, and I do have feelings. I lived with my mother and three sisters very briefly. This was a complex arrangement for me. My sisters used to make fun of my weight, which hurt my feelings. They would embarrass me in front of their friends and ridicule me by calling me names such as "a fat tub of lard" or "fat whale." Then they would laugh so hard because the spotlight was on me. I used to cry and act out because of how I was treated. I tried to endure the constant criticism; it was difficult, and I could not keep taking those hurtful remarks. My mother worked long hours because she was a single mother. I was a big baby and could not joke about their insecurities or hurt their feelings in return. As the youngest, I was not used to being treated this poorly when my parents were together. I did not know how to insult them, which frustrated me. I felt like they were winning, and I was the loser because I was young and inexperienced until I learned my strength, which was fighting.

This was my advantage, and this is how I solved any beef. I started using my fists to win against my sisters and anyone else who challenged me. I would fight when I was insulted or when my feelings were hurt. I did not know how to communicate my feelings, so I would fight. Once I started to use my hands to say the things that I could not, I noticed how good my fighting skills were. Then I fought my eldest sister, Paulette, and my sister had a reputation in the streets of Syracuse that she was not to be played with. When I won the fight with Paulette, I felt untouchable. So whenever I became offended, or someone crossed me, I would fight. I fought women, men, girls, and boys; it did not matter once they disrespected me.

Now, fighting with my sister Red was different. She was a lot smaller and good at using knives and razors. When we became adults, I teased my sister about how I taught her how to fight. My mom spanked me for my conduct. When she got off work, my mother cooked and fed me a good meal and told me to take my bath. I thought everything was okay since my father came to the school. However, it wasn't, and my mother ensured she set her precedence over what was expected of me in school. I began using my weight and size to my advantage; I was 5'9" and wore a size 7 or 8 women's shoe. Growing up, I always wore my age in shoe size, until I turned 12 years old. I had gotten taller, and I looked older than I was.

I still remember my dad cracking jokes about my feet. "Now, Melinda, if your feet keep growing, I'm going to tell the store just give me the boxes and they can keep the shoes." I still laugh at that joke today. My temper protected my vulnerability, and I became a beast in these streets when I became older. I learned how to use my mouth because I was a very wise young lady, and my hands had a reputation.

My anger had become more intense and deadly. I had learned to protect myself because of the lifestyle that I chose to live. At an early age, I had to be tough and a no-nonsense type of girl. At sixteen, I was on my own and caring for my father. I was making money both illegally and legally. I boot-legged liquor and sold weed, crack, and cocaine. So I had to handle myself on Syracuse's streets. I did not look for trouble. However, problems had their way of coming toward me.

I was a hustler, and I worked for myself. I looked out for those who I considered friends. That is how I was stabbed in my lower backside. My fat stopped the knife from piercing my kidney. This was done by a female whom I had let borrow money. I was shot at by a male, protecting my niece and her friend from a sexual assault. I had many other brawls, but this next battle led me to transformation. I disfigured a woman's face with a liquor bottle because she and my brother robbed my father's house. The woman came to my house to buy liquor and cigarettes from me after the robbery. I let her into my house and locked the door.

The woman was timid and pulled out a steak knife, and all I heard my homegirl say was, "Bitch you are going to jail!" I could not get to my brother because he hid from me. Yes, she pressed charges on me, and the police arrested me for an assault charge. During the arrest, they found a stolen assault rifle in my apartment, and I went to jail. I was on probation for some other minor changes that I had received.

When I was arrested, I violated probation and received new charges. I was looking at some jail time, and I had never done any significant prison time. I will never forget Honorable Judge Sandra Townes. Judge Townes was the woman who forced me to deal with myself, which ultimately helped me to change my life. Judge Townes made me sit with no bail or bond. I remember sitting for sixty days until she scheduled my next court date. I tried calling my probation officer, and she declined all my calls. I was forced to sit with myself and think about my life and how to overcome this obstacle I endured. It was not that I feared jail. I just could not fathom a person telling me what to do every waking moment of my time.

I remember sitting and writing my father because I did not have any friends who visited me during that time. They did not even bring me commissary down to the justice center. I remember my family coming to see me, and that is when my emotions came to the surface. I realized that I could not see them or my father. I was hurt because I could not be there for him. I remember my mother leaving me a prayer book. She told me to pray and ask God to help me. So I prayed, and I started going to church while I was incarcerated. One day a woman came to me and said, "Melinda, you put in a request to go to rehabilitation." I said, "Yes, I have an alcohol addiction. When I drink, my anger is out of control." The counselor listened and took notes. So by the time my court date came, I was set to go into Syracuse Behavioral Health Rehabilitation (SBH). I knew that working on myself would be the hardest thing to do then. However, I knew that I could not stay in jail.

I like challenges, and, in my opinion, doing jail time is not a challenge; it is a dictatorship. A person can ask me to do something, but to have power over when I eat, sleep, shower, and use the phone. No, I could not deal with that type of authority. I still owe the Justice Center money for a plastic chair that I broke because I got mad and smashed their chair. SBH helped to change my life for the better. The women who counseled me had been on my journey way before me, and they knew how to handle me. They understood that I was a beautiful mess, yet they challenged me and introduced me to another chance at living a blessed life. They dared me to become exceptional in all areas of my life.

Those counselors and the women I lived with for eight months pulled at areas of my life that others would not dare to address. These phenomenal women allowed me the space to start healing. They pulled the scab off the wound, which bled full of unresolved emotions: trauma, self-hatred, low self-esteem, anxiety, addiction to money, trust issues with women, unforgiveness, and motherly issues. They got to my source and helped me identify all my emotions. Once I identified the emotional pain and trauma feelings I carried around, they provided me with the tools to cleanse the wound of anger.

"Turn away from evil and do good; seek peace and pursue it" (Psalm 34:14, NKJV), and this is what I did. Through this rehabilitation program, I went through counseling and anger management counseling. Through anger management, I learned my ABCs: Actions, Behaviors, and Consequences resulting from my behavior. It took me five times to learn this concept, yet I learned. I realized that once I became accountable for my actions, I could change the outcome of my life. Transitioning required me to take an in-depth look at Melinda. I had to come to terms with my childhood trauma and other painful events that I had endured.

"But we all, with unveiled faces, beholding as in a mirror the glory of the Lord, are being transformed into the same image from glory to glory, just as from the Lord, the Spirit" (2 Corinthians 3:18, NKJV). Transformation requires a willingness to want to do better. My anger kept me from being successful in my early years. I was inexperienced in my thought process, especially in my twenties. My behavior has caused most of the financial strife I have endured. Due to my earlier lifestyle, which resulted in my criminal record, employers were skeptical about hiring a Black woman with a criminal record, and my height and weight did not help either.

I would not be surprised at how often I have been stereotyped by an employer. People currently label me. So I went back to school and acquired an understanding that has allowed me to continue the healing process within myself. Also, I fully understand the depth of my anger and how I am responsible for having control over my own emotions. Education has given me the tools to become my own patient. It is a human service saying that if you can't help yourself, how can you help the next person?

So it was not only my sisters ridiculing me that began to shape my anger. My family, environment, parents, and school helped shape my emotions. Anger is a scab that consists of unaddressed emotions, hurt, and painful experiences. These feelings had come into my life and left me vulnerable. "Never pay back evil for evil to anyone. Respect what is right in the sight of all men. So far as it depends on you, be at peace with all men. Never take your own revenge, beloved, but leave room for the wrath of God, for it is written, 'VENGEANCE IS MINE, I WILL REPAY,' says Lord" (Romans 12:17-21, NKJV). I swear it took me a long time to understand this verse and let it manifest in my life. When people used to hurt me, I wanted to make them feel how I felt. I wanted them to be in pain, and I wanted them to feel the hurt like me. Over the years, I had to learn that was not acceptable or healthy behavior. After finding God, I knew He did not want me to do as they did me. Yet, I constantly battled with my flesh for years and still get tested.

"And forgive us our debts, as we also have forgiven our debtors" (Matthew 6:12, NKJV). People say forgive others and release the toxins. It is difficult to forgive, especially starting out. However, it is necessary when you are manifesting change. I had to learn how to forgive others, but most importantly, I learned how to forgive myself. I had to let go of resentment toward myself for enduring the pain. I had to address the issues of how I longed for a relationship with my mother, especially during my adolescence and as a young adult. I had to forgive myself for being used and talked about amongst fake friends.

I had to let go of others' negative opinions about me and their deceitful ways that used to try to harm me. I had to release the abandonment issues, rejections, being socially awkward and allow myself to transform. A butterfly is a caterpillar at first, and then it goes through a transformation. I could not have transformed on my own. My mother introduced me to Christ. Even though our relationship had been challenged during my earlier years, I truly loved my mother, and I am thankful she introduced me to Jesus Christ, my Lord and Savior, and that through His grace, he allowed my incarceration. He allowed me time alone in that jail cell. Because during that time, he started planting a seed within me. That seed took over twenty-five years and a journey to bloom into fruition. This transformation has been in the works for years. I have experienced many hardships, and I have fallen many times. I tried throwing in the towel many times, but God threw the towel back and supplied me with His grace and mercy.

God allowed me to connect with two earth angels who are no longer amongst us. They taught me how to read the Bible for myself and showed me what unconditional love looked like and how unconditional love should feel. They also taught me how to have and sustain my personal relationship with God: my Pastor, Randolph Stackhouse, Jr. and First Lady Linda Stackhouse, may they both rest in paradise. They provided my children and me unconditional love and showed me how to raise my girls from a biblical standpoint. When I wanted to give up, my church family was behind me. When I needed guidance, God put people in my path to help me fulfill his purpose.

I feel like God chiseled away all that was tainted. He used the hardships in my life to mold and shape me. He allowed me to endure situations such as my children being taken from my custody to show me humility. He allowed a woman to repeatedly have me arrested on false charges and put me on administrative leave from my job to learn how to effectively advocate for myself. God has allowed people that I loved with all my heart to destroy mine and walk out on me. God intentionally prepared me for his purpose in life. The anger I endured as a child helps me understand my own children's anger.

"When I was a child, I talked like a child, thought like a child, and reasoned. When I became a man, I put the ways of childhood behind me" (1 Corinthians 13:11, NKJV). I grew up and no longer wanted to be an angry Black woman. Therefore, I had to change my way of thinking. I came to realize that I have control over Melinda. I do not have control over others. Then I started arming myself with mental strategies that would allow me control over any situation that triggered my anger. I currently arm myself with emotional tricks that will assist me when people push my limits. Over the years, I have revamped and revised my strategies and techniques. I have a solid, spiritual, and powerful network of people that I will call to help me deescalate in an emergency. The more arsenal that you have, the more successful outcomes you will experience. When you're dealing with yourself in any capacity, you must take time to learn and love yourself. Be patient with yourself and allow the Spirit to work within you.

I tell myself daily that I did not get like this overnight. These were years of neglect that I inflicted upon myself. Therefore, it will take time to repair the years of all this trauma and pain. But I can say in it all, God never took his hands off me. There have been some difficult times, yet he did not allow the trajectories to harm me. Today, I feel so much better and at peace. I still have challenging times and cross paths with difficult people. However, I am the one that is in control, and I will not allow anyone to steal my joy.

Through my journey, I have been in constant transformation for some time. Yet I have developed in ways only my personal experiences could have shown me. I was like a piece of wood; God was the artist who chiseled away all my inequities. Also, he showed me how to take what others looked at as a weakness and use it for good. The Spirit led me to use my vulnerability for his purpose. So what caused me to lose employment opportunities, acquire a negative character, and be adversely stereotyped allowed God to equip me to be used for his glory and to show others how He can manifest in their lives.

I have transitioned from that cocoon as the butterfly. My wings have spread my truth to help the next child, adult, or family understand that they too can overcome their anger. No, I did not overcome my bitterness in a short amount of time. I worked at it and made it a priority in my life. I wanted to be different and remove myself from people, places, and things to achieve this newfound peace. I am still a work in progress, and I am still actively working on my anger. I learn to recognize my triggers with every person I encounter and focus on what I can control. People are going to be people, and we all have choices. I value my choices, time, and energy.

I set healthy boundaries where I did not have any in the past. My consequences for no boundaries led me to befriend people with whom I had no business connecting, in relationships with spiritually dead people and not being obedient to God's word. However, I believe God used those instances for the glory of his purpose.

In conclusion, we all become angry, and anger is a normal human emotion formed from other negative emotions that we hurt by. However, we must release that anger in a way that we do not hurt another person or ourselves.

Anger is a poison that ultimately hurts and hinders us. To release the venom, we must address that underlying pain, and we do this by releasing the emotions. All these emotions are tied to mental health issues. So once we can become truthful with ourselves, we can begin to heal. Healing comes from being honest and having healthy connections with ourselves and others. As soon as I confronted the ugly truths that had held me back for so long, I began to heal. As I started the recovery, I began to forgive myself and those who hurt me. Then once I forgave, I started to love myself for all my flaws.

Romans 8:26, NKJV, says that the Spirit helps us in our weakness: "For we do not know what to pray for as we ought, but the Spirit himself intercedes for us with groanings too deep for words." Therefore, managing your anger is possible with faith and the willingness on your behalf to change. Change for me did not happen overnight. This transformation has been in effect for over twenty-five years. I just did not give up, even when times became hard.

I kept going even with tears in my eyes. I wanted to do and be better. I understood life was like being in constant trouble with the law and living life raucously. I wanted to experience making my parents proud and being approved by my family.

Our anger is a part of who we are. However, we can refuse to let our anger define us, and then we will be able to define and release those toxic emotions. When you release those negative feelings, you will have more room for your positive sentiments to distribute. Every day will not be peaceful and great. However, you will begin to block out negativity and create your own happiness.

This will happen by associating yourself with those who are positive, cutting out people, places, and things that no longer serve your purpose in life. For example, you hang around messy people. Now we all know some people who live for chaos and drama-filled lives—the people who sit around and talk down about everyone and share the secrets they know about everyone. Yes, those messy people you befriended to get the latest scoop on mutual associates. So when you are changing your life, you start examining the people you associate with and ask yourself if they are an asset or liability to your life. Do the people that I am around help to elevate me by educating me in areas so that I can prosper? Or are they draining me of my time, resources, and energy?

Then you start the elimination process. This practice is not easy and can be the most difficult. Anyone who has done inner work and progressed into a better person understands this. People who know the old you do not want you to change. They see your transformation as a threat to their connection on their dependency on you. If you and your associate used to gossip, they also knew people and your business. So if you change and stop gossiping about others with the associate, now the associate does not have the benefit of knowing your business, and they have lost a gossip buddy. You have changed for the better, and now you leave your associate to question themselves on their morals and values and what makes them so comfortable downplaying others. When you transform into a better version of yourself, you view others and the world in a healed sense. You learn to discern others' actions. When a person has inner turmoil, they behave differently than someone on the journey of healing. The individual undergoing a healthy transformation cannot see themselves in the unhealed person, because they are in tune with facing their own inner demons and transforming for the better. The healed individual recognizes all these patterns. The healthy person will utilize the personal arsenal that they have developed while transforming themselves. They will use techniques that will assist them in overcoming the negative person's tests. They will not entertain or associate with negative behaviors that they overcame.

However, a healthy person will help you recognize the stages by educating you and helping you identify those negative traits. For example, this chapter explains how a person learns how to control anger. I have overcome many legal and family struggles. I had encounters with the legal and family systems on my transformational journey. This has allowed me to examine my innermost being and account for my conduct. This has resulted in my recent transformation. Also, I gained the ability to help others, support them, and educate them to overcome their anger, because anger is a normal human emotion, controllable by the person experiencing the anger. All the individual needs is education and assistance in this process of healing. Then you can be on the journey of controlling your temper.

First, I would like to dedicate this chapter to Jesus Christ, the head of my life. I want to thank God for instilling the obedience to fulfill his purpose. I also would like to thank those who pushed me to tell a part of my story so that it may help someone else. Next, I want to shout out to my fur baby Royalty Queen. When I first started writing my chapter, she would sit right under me while I typed my story out, up until her passing. Royalty showed me the true meaning of unconditional love, and I will forever miss my pup.

Lastly, I want to thank my three children and my mom. I began understanding the importance of breaking generational traumas while composing my chapter. It is essential to cultivate generational love and abundance because those bonds carry over to the next generation.

I want to thank my best friend Rebecca for her encouragement, uplifting messages, unconditional love, and overall support. Thank you, Eric and Dionne Wagner, for allowing me to mention the First Lady and Pastor Stackhouse in my story; it meant a lot because they were such big supporters of my children and me. This was indeed a blessed experience, and I pray I helped at least one person. Thank you for reading my chapter. May my words provide encouragement to transform your life.

"When you choose to forgive those who have hurt you, you take away their power."

Anonymous

Sherry S. Beam is a #1 Amazon bestselling author of *I Rise Living, Beyond the Bruises*. She is also a certified Domestic Violence Help Coach. Sherry is a survivor of domestic violence, which led her to take a course to further be able to assist other victim's, to break the bondage's that holds them captive.

Sherry found her purpose and her mission. She is licensed to facilitate a program to help victims reclaim their voice and take back their lives, to help alleviate the shame and pain of the past and begin living in their God given destiny.

Sherry lives in Charlotte, North Carolina surrounded by her six children and grandchildren. She enjoys being involved in her community events and charities. She loves walking for cancer, lupus and aids research.

CHAOS BREAKING FAITH

Sherry S. Beam

"*Now faith is the substance of things hoped for, the evidence of things not seen.*" Hebrews 11:11, KJV

"I must be dreaming; please God, tell me I'm dreaming. Wake me out of this horrible vision." Standing here feeling a gut-wrenching scream trying to emerge from my lips, I wanted to run but I couldn't move. I felt paralyzed. I was gazing at a small boy lying in the street. He remained lifeless, eyes set and fixed, looking toward the sky. There was a massive amount of blood running from the back of his injured head into the culvert. The child lying in the street was my youngest child, my baby. "Dear sweet Jesus, help me! You're the only name I know to call on."

This was the last of a series of tragic events that happened in 1993. This all transpired within a five-month span of time. Was there an assignment from hell loosed on my life? Had there been word curses spoken against me? "Lord, Father, this one is too hard to bear, I need you." You see, if this had occurred three years prior, I don't know what the outcome would have been. At that point in my life I was a broken vessel, still grieving the death of my mother from years before. She had been such an inspiration in my life, a woman of strong faith.

I had faith, but going through trials after my mother passed, I figured out it was her spiritual coattail I had been holding onto. I had gleaned from her knowledge and understanding, but I truly hadn't developed my own faith. We are all given a measure of faith (*Romans 12:3*). We have to cultivate and nurture that faith in order for it to take root. We grow from faith to faith (*Romans 1:17*). There is a process we go through to grow that kind of faith, to trust in God and His word. This would be my growing season.

At this juncture in life I'd been married for nineteen years. It started declining after seven years, yet I held on. I prayed for a turnaround, to no avail. The marriage became more dysfunctional and abusive. After enduring physical and emotional abuse for a length of time, it took its toll on my mind and body. I became enshrouded in darkness and a web of lies tormented me day and night. To alleviate the pain, I began to drink alcohol.

I could hear voices saying, "You're no good, you're a bad wife and mother, you can't do anything right, you're better off dead." Where once faith thrived, the enemy of my soul had planted lies. Subconsciously, I began to believe them, to the point of contemplating suicide. I was at a crossroad; I had to make a choice. The battle raging between life and death rang louder and louder in my mind, "You'd be better off dead."

I sat crying, thinking of my loveless marriage, the humiliation I'd endured, longing for the advice and arms of my mom. I decided that night to end my suffering. I planned to overdose myself and slice my wrist to find peace. As things were set in motion, I glimpsed a picture of mom on a shelf, then my Bible. Something snapped within, and I cried out. Why had I let the lies that crept in unaware almost cause destruction?

We need to be aware of our thoughts at all times. *2 Corinthians 10:5* tells us to take them captive and pull them down to the obedience of Christ. I'd been so focused on my pain and grief my faith had waned. The lessons I'd been taught and having seen the hand of God move in my life in earlier years, they had dwindled. I cried out to the only one I knew who could deliver me. "Jesus, I ask you to take me, cleanse me of all the hurt and pain. Take the grief and bitterness from my soul; make me whole, Lord."

As soon as the prayer rolled from my lips, I fell to my knees. There was a warm feeling that enveloped me inside and out. It felt as if water was flowing over me. Kneeling there that night brought deliverance and my faith was restored. My walk in life was changed forever. I grew stronger in my faith and in who I am in Christ. I set boundaries in my life that were nonnegotiable. I obtained a position with a company, was promoted three times within six months by the grace of God, and I was personnel manager. I truly thanked God for my peace and freedom to be me. Even though I was still married, I gave it to God. I asked him to remove any stumbling blocks that kept me from Him.

After two years of walking by faith, it would be challenged. My world would begin to spin out of control. I received a frantic call from my sister. Our dad had suffered a heart attack and stroke. He was being rushed to Charlotte from the neighboring county where he resided. Another sister and I had made our way to the hospital. After exams and being settled in his room, the doctors came in and said Dad was in dire condition. Their prognosis was Dad would not survive the night. My spirit man would not accept this; it wasn't fleshly out of my emotions. My spirit said, "Pray," so my sister and I did just that. Even though they told us we couldn't stay at Dad's bedside, we received permission to remain in the waiting room for intensive care. We prayed for covering over Dad, attending doctors, and nurses—prayers of protection and healing emitted from that room most of the night.

As we were awakened by nurses, we rushed to Dad's room, where we were greeted by a big, beautiful smile and "What do you have for me" from him. Dad was sitting upright and eating. The doctors were amazed at his recovery and had no explanation. Dad's response was, "I know a man" and he pointed upward. "Hallelujah!" I could only dance and I didn't care who saw me. We have to flex our muscles of faith, even in the small things we go through. Don't wait until a catastrophe to find your legs. That night was a booster cable to my faith. Little did I know, I would need it for what was coming my way.

Dad went home from the hospital the last week in July of 1993. Almost two weeks later my sister was admitted. She lived in Charlotte, about six blocks from me. There wasn't a day that went by where we didn't see each other. That weekend we had a birthday party for one of our kids. Her mouth started hurting and we found out she had been suffering with a toothache for over three weeks. She had antibiotics prescribed to her from the dentist, but she was in excruciating pain. Before I left her, I made her promise if she felt any worse, she would go to the emergency room. She promised and I left for work. I worked third shift and was extremely tired when I arrived home. My boys were up getting ready for school. I got them out the door and began preparing for bed.

Before I got to my bedroom, there was a knock at the door. My goddaughter was there to inform me the ambulance had taken my sister to the emergency room. Okay, she promised me she would call the medic if she got worse. I thought to myself, *She's all right now; she'll get treatment and will recover like new*, but my spirit said stay awake. As soon as I turned around from locking the door another knock came. My sister from Lincolnton came in. She had been to the hospital and said sis was in ICU—for a toothache? I thought something was off about this. She said she was going back to Lincolnton to give a report about the situation to our dad and would return later. I felt like I should bathe and get dressed.

As soon as I got dressed there was a loud bang at the door. It was my niece and her boyfriend screaming, "We need to get to the hospital now." By the time we made it my sister had passed away. The same sister who had lamented all night for our father was gone. The doctors hadn't told her children, even though all of them were over twenty, except the two younger ones in school. How could I tell them? I was in disbelief myself. "Oh Lord, what about Dad?" All I could do was call on Jesus. "I need your peace and strength right now." The nurse pulled me aside and stated that she believed my sister knew she was leaving because she had asked her to remain in the room because she didn't want to die alone.

Her children were devastated, Dad was shaken, and I had to stop him just before he was opening the door to her room. We sat him down to explain to him of her demise. The infection in her mouth had erupted and spread through her body; her organs had shut down. We were all staring at one another, at a loss for words. That night as I lay awake, I cried in agony. She was my sister, my friend, the one who understood me best, as I understood her. "Lord, grant us your strength and peace to brave this unexpected storm surrounding her children and Dad especially. Let them embrace your love and relieve them of their pain as only you can do."

I can truly say God kept me through it all. His love engulfed me as I cried myself to sleep night after night. I went through the process to release my grief to Jesus. "He is my rock and my fortress, my deliverer, my God, my strength, in whom I will trust, my buckler and the Lord of my salvation, and my high tower" (Psalm 18:2).

We'll be stretched in ways we don't understand, yet in that stretching, our faith is increasing. The more I lean in and trust God, the more I learn to handle. My sister passed away on August 10, 1993, almost two weeks after Dad's episode. It was also the day our mother died eight years prior. I began to dread that day. God revealed a seed of fear that had been planted when I started questioning the cause of my anxiety during this time. That lying spirit tried to take a foothold again. I started fighting back with the word now, casting down those imaginations I saw it work to dismantle the fear. "Yes, Lord." I had gone back to work a week after the funeral to the new manager's arrival from Chicago. There was an atmosphere of oppression lingering. The present manager pulled me aside privately; his words were "watch your back." They had secretly come in and replaced him; all of the other staff figured they would be replaced also. My heart was at rest. "The Lord brought me here and he will provide when I leave" was my sentiment. Later on I would realize God's plan. I lost my job but fought for my unemployment benefits. The company tried to deny them, but I won. The week after I left the whole company was dismissed from the building. What they meant for evil God turned around for my good.

The end of September the same year a police car pulled up. I was confused because I hadn't called and all of my boys were in school, or so I thought. My middle son had been in an accident at school. The police were there to rush me to the hospital. As I entered the room, I gasped, trying to hold back the scream. My son's femur was broken and his knee was out of place, almost protruding through his skin. Papers were signed and he was rushed into emergency surgery. I felt numb, sitting and waiting for what seemed like an eternity, trying to keep control of my imagination. The doctors finally emerged with good news; he was stable. They were able to mend the knee and leg. He had pins and rods, but all went well. He had a cement cast from his ankle up to his thigh.

I hadn't had time for grief, a pity party or just to sit and take a deep breath, moving from one tragedy to the next. "Lord, I place my all into your hands; I surrender all. With all that is happening, am I being cursed, is someone wishing evil upon us? I dare not react out of flesh. Lead me, Lord, through it all."

Am I saying your walk will be easy? Certainly not. We all have challenges; it's how we go through them that determines our outcome. Through my journey I've learned to rely on sound instructions, to lean on the wisdom found there. When I do it my way, lots of times I've suffered mistakes. Proverbs 3:6, tells me to acknowledge my ways and He will direct my path. Like I said, it's a process. I think this is His will for me to get angry, to go to a certain place, give away something, whatever. Doing things my own way had me repeating cycles. I learned to trust and believe it's not over; we go from faith to faith. Me being fired was a blessing in disguise. I was able to remain at home to attend to my son, to make sure he was comfortable, because with the heavy cast he couldn't even turn himself. I was able to pay bills because my unemployment checks arrived on time. God knew what we needed.

On November 13, about a month later, I woke up with an eerie feeling. Something just didn't feel right; what was it? The boys were clothed, fed and off to school. I began cleaning the house, helping my son bathe and positioning him so he could watch television. The feeling continued as if a warning. I couldn't shake it all day. "Lord, what is this?" That afternoon my baby was hit by a car. They never stopped once, they hit him with full force, and they tried to leave him lying in the street until people started screaming to stop her. His father rode in the ambulance as they sped to the trauma center. My brother-in-law rushed me there. As I ran through the doors of the emergency room, I noticed the two officers that were at the scene. One turned his head, his hand covering his face; the other one stood there with red eyes and a tear-stained face. A nurse approached me, asking if I was the mother. I almost collapsed. I pleaded for them to take me to my son, and I was escorted to another waiting area. No sign of my husband. My brother-in-law left to go alert the rest of the family before it was on the news.

I sat alone, the scene playing over and over in my mind: the blood, his eyes in a blank stare, the medic frantically performing CPR; he was finally intubated in the middle of the street. Feelings of helplessness and guilt flooded through me because I couldn't help my child. I just wanted to be able to hold him tight right now and tell him how much I loved him. A nurse and patient representative approached me; behind them I noticed the chaplain. They wanted to talk with me, I thought to give me an update. The patient representative motioned to a door. When I turned, shock and panic gripped me instantly; it was the same room only three months ago they ushered us into to inform us that my sister had passed away. Before I could contain myself, I dropped to my knees, screaming, "No, no, I won't go in there." I asked them to just take me to my son. By that time other family members had made it here. It was six hours before I would even know if my child had survived.

I braced myself before I walked into his room. He was on life support. Never in my life had I witnessed a sight like this. Tubes were all in his little body, screws drilled into his skull to let the pressure off his brain. The left side of his face, the top layer of the skin was completely gone. Tears rolled down my face as I made my way to his bedside. I leaned down and kissed him and whispered to him, "Mommy's here." I refused for him to hear me break down when he needed me. The doctors met us in the waiting room. Their report was my baby was hit so hard that his brain twisted in his skull. His skull fractured when he hit the street, and he was having seizures. My only question was, "What are my son's chances of living 70/30? 60/40? What?" Nine out of ten doctors dropped their heads. The neurosurgeon stated, "There is so much damage to his brain there is no way I can see where to begin." There was a pause in his statement; he then added, "All I can tell you is to pray."

When he said that it felt as if someone pushed me in my back. I had to catch myself as I rocked forward, then I heard a small voice: "You know what to do." I looked around at everyone. I knew it was time to fight. I made an announcement to my family. No one was to enter into his room with any doubt or unbelief, no screaming or crying. Go in his room and pray with him, talk to him as if he's coming home. The doctors weren't even allowed to talk about his condition in the room. I took a position in the corner of the waiting room. I prayed there each time after visiting my son. One day I asked God, "Father, if you let my son live even if I have to change his diapers for the rest of his life, I'll gladly do it." I heard, "I'll do that and more." After two weeks and still in a coma, the doctors decided it was time to pull the plug. There was no hope or improvement as they saw. I still prayed and believed God's promise. He shall not die, but live and declare the works of the Lord (Psalm 118:17).

As they began removing the tubes, preparing for him to go to the morgue, God was faithful. My son's heart, lungs and kidneys started functioning on their own. He lay in a coma until New Year's Day. Our family and friends all over, people overseas prayed corporately for him on New Year's Eve. That morning I walked into the room, and the nurse stopped me at the door. "Can you call his name?" she said, so I did. Where there was a blank stare the day before, my baby turned his head toward my voice. I screamed, "Hallelujah" and broke out praising God. If I had believed the lie, instead of God...He wouldn't let us fall. He was in the hospital a total of four months and two weeks before going home. Where his left side was totally paralyzed, there is only some weakness in the arm. He is walking, talking, and giving me a run for my money.

There has never been a complaint coming from his mouth, only, "Mom, you know God saved me and did not let me be dragged under that car." Never give up hope. From faith to faith we see the salvation of the Lord.

Deborah Annette Maddox is a photographer and a graphic designer. Her company's name is iAmblessed 17 Photography. The picture tells the story in more ways than one. No matter what she looks at through the lens, she is able to consistently see the essence of the picture that is being taken.

Deborah is a wife, mother, grandmother, and great-grandmother. She has been given the ability to assist her family, friends, and others who have entered her life. As a result, she has assisted children who were in need and later became a foster mother to several of them.

Deborah pursued furthering her education to receive a bachelor's degree in business administration and general management. She had a loving assignment for the last six years, and that was to provide care for her mother-in-law until the day of her passing. Her gift is to be a nurturer and to assist in any way possible.

CONNECTING THE DOTS HIS WAY, NOT MINE

Deborah Maddox

When trying to connect the dots in life, you may find that many have been left out. It's like being born again. We all know how we got here, but the question is how can one go through the process a second time? Sometimes our way of thinking has caused the entire image to be completely thrown out of whack. As a result, there are defects, errors, and even troubles with the image. We often ask ourselves, how can they be fixed? After connecting the dots in my life, I have been shown my own image from the beginning to the present. Though the entire 27th Psalm is my favorite, Proverbs 3:5-6 has walked me throughout while connecting me to where God wants me to be.

"Trust in the LORD with all thine heart; and lean not unto thine own understanding. In all thy ways acknowledge him, and he shall direct thy paths"

I am the second oldest child of Izetta and the late James Taylor. As a small child, I learned that I was the questioning one. I didn't take no for an answer. When they said no, I found ways around it to make things happen. I found that this trait has followed me into adulthood, which is not a bad trait to have. Growing up with three brothers, I had to be tough. Our parents were workaholics. They didn't say much about love. It was an action word for them. Their actions spoke louder than words, but back in those days, it would have been good to hear the words. Looking back to connect the dots, I found some were imperfect. As a result, I never wanted to follow my parents' footsteps, but in some ways I did.

Being my parents' wild child, I wanted to know about the things they weren't willing to share in my childhood home. I learned through my life's journey with my parents that what I was curious about as a young child wasn't talked about in our home nor in theirs either. That was a generation of "do as I say and not as I do," better known as children were seen and not heard. So we followed suit for generations, trying to connect the dots. Through my life's journey, I never wanted to hurt people but ended up being the one that got hurt. I was always looked over, interrupted, or simply not acknowledged during conversations, which made me feel hurt and as if no one was listening. It was as if my conversation didn't matter.

As a small child I was pushed to the side. There's something about being raped or molested. It's a violation because someone took something from you without your permission. It runs through your mind for years, and you have no idea why. Someone taking something from you is stealing. They stole it without your consent, not knowing the damage it would cause. In my opinion, it was as if they didn't care.

As a young child and even into adulthood, I ran from arm to arm. It felt like how a baby feels being passed around until you get to the right arms. Looking and wanting to be loved is what many of us long for. I know I did. I thought my path of ignoring the pain, moving on with my life, and pretending it never happened was an endpoint, but I was wrong. That's what I did. Just covered it up and kept moving. Don't talk about it because it would only bring more trouble. Sometimes it felt like a cut; I would wipe it off, then put a band-aid on it and over time it would heal, or not. I learned that some cuts or wounds needed to be aired out.

My first child came at the age of sixteen. I just wanted to give and receive love in return. I received broken promises from the father, but one thing he did state was that he would only marry the woman who had his son. Well, marriage wasn't in our cards because I had a girl. As I connect those dots to back then, I thought he was the one. That image was messed up due to being too young and not in God's will. As for my journey in life, I had to move from the Albany area due to him trying to control me and not allowing me to have other relationships. I remember him being with whomever he wanted, but for me that wasn't the case. I was young and wanted to be with him, but he didn't want me. After coming to the realization that I couldn't have him, I prayed to ask God what my next step was. At the age of seventeen, I took a leap of faith by leaving the Albany area with my daughter. In my faith walk, we ended up in Syracuse.

Syracuse became our new home. My mother and two brothers were already there because she received a job transfer. Once getting established, I knew staying with my mother was out of the question because I walked to the beat of my own drum. I now had a child to raise, and my mother had already mentioned that I made that bed, so I needed to lie in it. That child was my responsibility, not hers. Everything she said was correct. I was responsible for this little person. As I connected the dots to this image, I had to ask myself, "Where is the manual that will guide me to make whatever decisions I need to make concerning me and this little person?" No manual came out with her when she came into this world. I went to church, read my Bible, and prayed, but I had one foot in and one foot out.

Now, in the eyes of society, I was grown with a child. I had to start making grown decisions whether I wanted to or not. So I set out looking for a job, which turned out to be at Burger King on the east side of Syracuse. After being there for a while, a woman by the name Helen asked me a question: "What are the plans you have for your life?" My response to her was to work and raise my daughter. Then she stated I needed to do a self-evaluation. Well, after doing a self-evaluation, I realized I was a teenage mother with no education. After connecting the dots, reality kicked in. The image that I had wasn't going to work. Being a high school dropout with a child—how far would that get me? Not far at all. I made up my mind that I was going back to school. After re-enrolling in school, I started going through this program that would either help me get my GED or put me back into the general school population.

After being at Nottingham, I made up my mind that I wanted a diploma, so that's what I set out to get. I worked, went to school, and took care of my daughter. In the midst of me getting my life into some type of order and figuring it out, one day, my daughter came home from daycare sick. I took her to her pediatrician at Saint Joseph's for them to give me a diagnosis that she just had a very bad cold. Well, she had more than a cold – she had stopped eating and we couldn't break her fever. We took her to Crouse to learn that she had pneumonia in three places in her lungs. I wouldn't leave her. I stayed and slept under the crib, praying and talking to my heavenly Father. For seven days, I parked in the same spot. She was in this bubble with tubes running all over the place. "But God." Once she was out of the hospital, I went back to getting things done. Corporate America will call it getting back to business as usual. After being with my mom for one year, I moved out to my first apartment, which was called Hilltop. We moved into the 1815 building on the Hill, Apt 3A. On my own, I figured it out by going through the motions trying to connect the dots.

My mother didn't want us to leave, but I didn't want to be under anyone else's rules. Her main reason for not wanting me to leave was that I wouldn't complete what I started because of past behaviors and people I associated myself with. My mother and my brothers ended up leaving Syracuse. I didn't go because I was determined to prove them wrong. They said I was going to follow my mother and would continue to be in her shadow. After connecting those dots, I learned that you couldn't make it without an education, and I couldn't follow my mother because God had a different plan for me. While still working for Burger King, taking care of my daughter, and completing my education, I got my diploma. Things started to come through for me until the man I was seeing left, and then my first apartment went up in flames, I lost everything, but the most important thing was that I didn't lose my life or the lives of the people who were in the apartment with me.

I was crippled at the fact that I had to start over, not knowing which direction I was about to go. Everything was lost but what we had on our backs. We had our lives; I still had my job, but all my stuff was gone, causing me to start over. After the hotel stays that the Red Cross provided ran out, I decided to send my daughter to my mother and stay behind to rebuild. As I connect the dots, I should have left too. Nope, pride got in the way. I was determined to make it and not to be in my mother's shadow or to follow her. My choices, my life. Well, while working from sunup to sundown trying to figure it out, one of my ex-boyfriend's mothers allowed me to sleep on her couch. After being on her couch for several months, she called me in to have a talk. This talk would remind me that stuff can be replaced, but life couldn't, and my daughter couldn't live with my mother forever. After the talk, reality set in. I made a promise to my daughter that I would be back to get her. It was temporary, not permanent.

After waking and making a few calls, God began to show me what was next. I was blessed with a three-bedroom apartment in

Housing. While working at the Post Standard newspaper, new dots began to formulate a new image. I met a woman by the name of Sandra. She didn't pull any punches and gave me some additional nuggets. In life, I needed to stop, think, and then go. That to me signified a traffic light because anything I said out of my mouth wasn't going to work. With all that was going on, I had to see my life in a whole new way. We lost everything, but our lives weren't lost. I decided to visit Tucker Missionary; one thing I can say is that even though I wasn't consistently in the building, I never stopped praying because I knew where my help came from, and it wasn't man. I only visited there for a short time, then I stopped.

Later in the year, I went to a hotel party with a few of the girls and met a soldier who became my husband ten months after we met each other. Looking back at those dots, we didn't really know each other. It was just for security. He needed someone to be there in case something happened while he was on deployment, and I just needed security. We grew to love each other, but we weren't in love with each other. I later left my job at the newspaper company to work at the bank. There came another part of my grooming. Ms. P was the branch manager, who ran a tight ship. One day, I got called into her office; our talk was about my attire. She asked if I was coming to work or going to a club. After leaving her office, thoughts began to run through my mind. What impression was I giving off? More of the dots were being formed. If you want to be treated like you are in a club, you will dress like you are in one and pick up whatever comes through the door. But if my attire was work attire, I would be all about business. It was not only a reference to my work life, but it had to do with my overall life as well. The branch closed and I had to find another job. We had to move from one section of housing to another for renovations. I went to work at a gas station and the dots really became real.

Yes, I was still married to the soldier, but he was still married to the club life and everything that came with it. We only had a weekend marriage. From time to time, I would travel to go see him. The soldiers had a code they would use if the wife entered the club and they were with other women. So on a particular night, I went to surprise him but got surprised. He wasn't in the barracks. He and a group of others traveled to Canada. I stayed with one of his boys, who was also married but had company who wasn't his wife. The next morning, I got home and stated to myself, "What's good for the goose is good for the gander." He didn't take our marriage seriously, and neither did I. So I found myself running again to cover up the hurt and pain.

He called one weekend and said he wasn't coming home. So a group of us went to Rochester for a Biggie concert. The auditorium was full. Everyone was smoking weed. I so wanted to fit in, so I asked if I could hit it too. It only took one puff! Oh my goodness, I thought it was regular weed, but oh boy, I found out it was chocolate-Thai. Well, this chocolate left me high for seven days. The seven-day high prompted me to pray, asking God to bring me down, and if he did, he would never have to worry about me touching it again. Things come to teach us lessons, and this one I learned quickly. This change caused me to go back to church, and my life began to change.

I put my marriage on the line, praying to God that if this is the man for me, let him stand on His foundation, but if not, remove him in Jesus' name. Time went on and things remained the same, nothing changed. This particular week was our third-year wedding anniversary and his class reunion. To him, the only thing that mattered was his class reunion. I asked him to wait until Thursday so we could all go together, but he and my daughter traveled without me. When he left, my last words were not good. I told him not to let a tragedy happen because this was not the way I wanted to meet his family. We had been married for three years and I had never met his family. Remember, we got married on the fly, not because we loved each other, but for security.

With all the hurt brewing inside looking at these dots in this image, I no longer wanted to be alone. Marriage wasn't supposed to be like this, so I decided that when the weekend came, I would go out with a friend to a local bar. There was no smoking involved, but this night, alcohol was my poison. I said to myself, "I don't care what happens to him." The only thing I wanted was to get my daughter back. That night I got wasted trying to wash everything away. The friend I went out with didn't want me to go home by myself. So before she brought me home, we went to breakfast. After getting home in bed, my phone rang and the person on the other end stated that my husband had been in a life-threatening car accident. I told the person to stop playing on my phone and then hung up. My phone rang two more times with different people calling to say the same thing. By the third call, I was on the phone making the necessary calls to find out what was going on.

These dots caused me to go back down on my knees to do a retraction, asking the Lord to forgive me and to save his life. This image was so unexpected, and I learned that life and death are in the power of your tongue. I wanted a changed man, not a dead man. Now God showed me His power. Not knowing how in the world I would get to Alabama or what I would be facing once I got there, I just stayed in continuous prayer. Since he was in the military, they contacted me, stating my flight had been booked. I was on my way to face whatever it was. I called the friend I went out with, and we prayed. Once I got to the airport, I met a pastor and I asked him to put my husband on the altar. But before we departed to get on our flight, we prayed right there in the airport.

Once I got to Alabama's airport, I was greeted by two people holding a sign. All they kept saying was "you are so beautiful." All that was playing in my mind was that I didn't want to meet his family this way. We had about a two-hour drive to get to where he was. On our arrival at the hospital, I was greeted by at least twenty to thirty people, along with my daughter, not knowing any of them except for my daughter. My words to them were, "It's nice to meet you all, but I need to see my husband." I was on a mission, and I would meet and greet after seeing him. Totally not knowing what I was about to see, one of his cousins took me to the ICU floor.

Getting to the ICU floor and seeing him lying there, I began to pray to ask God for his guidance. Next, I called for the nurse because I had a lot of questions and asked that he get cleaned up; there was dry blood in his ears, along with particles from the car still on his body. Last, I stopped all traffic going in and out of his room. These dots to this image taught me to be careful what I ask for, as well as how to deal with unforgiveness from childhood to the present situation. During this time, a lot was going through me. I did go down and meet and talk to his family. The family I told him I didn't want to meet due to tragedy. They were all surprised because they thought he was lying about having a wife. Some of them knew about me, but others didn't. I received an offer to go stay at one of their homes, but my mission was to be by my husband's side for however long it would be.

I slept in the hospital waiting room day in and day out, waiting for change to happen. My routine was morning, afternoon, and evening prayer with scripture, along with receiving updates on his condition. People would stop by to see him or call, and the question asked would be, "Would you like to pray?" My response would be "YES!" The connection of these dots was like no other, seeing God at work and believing in the midst of this storm. One day, while I was reading the scripture over him, a man approached me and told me to ask God to give my husband life and breath again, and that I needed to forgive past hurts and the stuff I was holding on to. This was the image changer. The dots that were given made a statement. Be specific in what you are asking God for, along with forgiving others. So I did. Every time a prayer was said over him, I incorporated the scripture. It convicted me to the point where I called my parents and asked them for their forgiveness. I was making my request known until the Lord showed me results for my repentance.

I began to see the change happening before my eyes. On the seventh day, they began to lower the induced coma medicine and he started to respond to current commands. His first words were that he had to go to the bathroom. I cried because I was seeing the miracle with my own eyes. It wasn't something that somebody told me, but something I witnessed. A few days later, I went to his hospital room earlier than normal to find a person wiping the bed he once lay in, so I began to cry. I cried out, "Lord, you promised!" and fell to my knees. The nurse ran into the room, stating he had been moved to a private room so I could sleep in the room with him. The waiting room had now come to an end, and the dots started to formulate an additional image – Standing on the Lord's promises and that he was a God who would not lie, no matter what the circumstances or situation.

I went back to the waiting room with tears running down my face and grabbed my suitcase. All I kept saying was "thank you, thank you, thank you." I was walking and rejoicing on my way to his new room. That morning, we began with prayer along with scripture, and after I was done, he responded, "Amen"—the dots that, no matter what, restored me from the hurt and fixed the pain through his love and his word. My husband had a long road ahead of him, and once he was well enough, the military flew him to Walter Reed to further assist in his recovery. So, in these dots of healing and forgiveness, it was beautiful until one day a call came through asking how he was doing, and I told her. One thing I explained to each caller was that he had associates before we met, so it was fine that she called and checked on him. I later found out she was a young lady from Canada. Once again, I was being tried, but I didn't buckle. She stated she wanted to come visit him. I told her it was a free country, and she could come as long as she respected me as HIS WIFE. I didn't care what happened before because God changed the image to look better than before. When you forgive a person, it can't be partial; it's all or nothing.

She tried to explain their relationship, but I asked him if he wanted to talk to her. His response was "no, and can you ask her to stop calling." I relayed the message, but she gave some choice words before hanging up. Those dots didn't match up for her—oh well, what God has for me is for me.

He had been at Walter Reed for an additional three months. After being discharged from the hospital, we moved to a townhouse in Liverpool. Then he received a full discharge from the military. His sister came to stay with us, and things started to go left. One day we were playing, and he snapped. He went from 0-to-100. He got upset and threw a hot iron at me. His sister and I had some choice words; he was on her side and not mine. After all this mess took place, I told him one day he would wake up and wish he still had me. He decided to go back to Alabama with his sister, and he then stayed for a while. Things definitely turned for the worse. His sister stated the reason she came was to take her brother back home.

The life we knew before showed back up. He wanted the old lifestyle and to be where his family was. *What are we?* I thought. I later moved back into the city and met a man who definitely changed my life. He became my best friend, and we started dating for five and a half years while I was still married to my first husband. How were these dots different from others? Well, he was an older man, but to us, age was just a number. He already had four children, and they had children, except for one of them. I only had one child, and I explained to him that I couldn't have any more because that's what I was told by the doctors. The first year we met, he asked me for a kiss. I told him no because I didn't know where his mouth had been. Homie don't play that. I later learned he went to church. That was definitely a plus. It might not have been every Sunday, but he was in the house, and he did visit the church I was attending when we first met.

I later left that church and started going back to Tucker Missionary. Pastor, J, counseled me regarding my first marriage. He asked me for a picture of my previous husband. We prayed, and God handled the rest. Once again, I found myself asking for direction. I wanted to be in good standing with God. My current husband and I would often talk about how God had changed his life. So he decided to rededicate his life to Christ—he got baptized as a grown man. Lord, not my will, but let your will be done. The connection was definitely different. We talked about marriage, and he said he wasn't getting married again. I remember stating I wouldn't submit to any man. Sometimes we are unaware of the things that come out of our mouths, but He is aware of the plans he has for us. Though there were similar things that rose up in our relationship, I went to God and prayed the same prayer. If this man be for me, let him stand on his foundation, but if not, remove him in the name of Jesus.

Looking back, connecting the dots on my first marriage as to why it didn't work, he wanted a different lifestyle that I was not willing to live. We never became one, and his immediate family was his only family. However, before our divorce, he stood up in the old church I attended and made a statement, "Don't run up to me and tell me what my wife has done because you don't know what I've been doing." We later divorced, and I remarried. In connecting the dots in my current marriage, we worked as a team. Is it perfect? No. Do we go through some things? Yes. Knowing that what

God has put together, let not man put asunder (Matthew.19:6). The Lord put two imperfect people together to show us how to make it work according to His will on one accord. Through my second marriage, the image of the dots became clearer. The blessing we received seven months after we were married was that God blessed my womb with a child. Doctors said I couldn't, but God said I could. In the past six years things have been thrown at me and I've wanted to throw in the towel. But the towel got thrown back and I was able to get my Associate's in graphic design and a bachelor's degree in business administration general management.

I even had to connect the dots when it came to this anthology project. I wanted to pass it off by giving it to someone else to avoid doing it and run thinking their message would be better received than mine. I've learned to reflect back on some encounters where the dots didn't make sense at the time, but they do now. I am chosen, and thankful for this opportunity to able to share my story. Remember in connecting the dots God's way, you will be able to see that no matter if you are broken, a misfit, mix-match, unsure, or have a disability, He has a purpose for you. You first must see yourself in His image.

Dedication

The assurance that God's word will not be rendered null or invalid. This chapter is devoted to all women who refuse to settle for less than they deserve, who won't rush into the wrong arms, and who understand their value. To my husband Edward Maddox II, my children, my family, as well as to late James Taylor Sr. my father, and mother-in-law Lula Donald, thank you for all your love and support.

Reverend Ardella Angela Young is the creator of Tranquil Rhythms S.P.A. (Spiritual Prosperity in Action) and Prodigal Daughter Ministries LLC. Her divine purpose and intention is to support, empower, and encourage the well-being and healing of individuals and groups who are seeking alternative methods to cope with grief; anger; trauma; addiction; social violence; emotional, physical, mental and verbal abuse; family dysfunction; LGBTQ; disassociation; and abandonment issues.

As a minister of spiritual consciousness and a spiritual life coach, Reverend Ardella supports those in the dark to find the light by finding and embracing an intimate relationship with God. She invites students to embrace a daily spiritual practice to align their thoughts and choices with spiritual laws and principles for a greater level of self-awareness. Providing opportunities for students to identify and release habitual patterns of behavior that impact their ability to live peacefully and to experience inner joy and freedom where unconditional self-love, self-acceptance, and self-appreciation occurs naturally.

Reverend Ardella facilitates workshops on Trust, Forgiveness, and Inner child work. She is a faith-based counselor, a breath-work consultant, reiki practitioner, and an employee of God.

One of her favorite sayings is, "I am here only to be who I am, to be my Self, which is Love."

Namaste!

UNFINISHED

Rev. Ardella Angela Young

Introduction Chronicles

1. Easy Does It

This cliché has always seemed to be misinterpreted as don't do anything. Just chill, and life will take care of itself. In the recovery arena, I construed these words as a way to calm someone down, in a midst of a breakdown, a bout of anger or feeling the need to overcompensate, which I can relate to. The true meaning, what I am to understand is, to get honest with self after discovering the mental or emotional difficulty and to believe and trust that where I am in that moment is where I work from. Be it a word, a phrase, or a sentence at a time, I have learned to sit with, let it resonate with me, and most important is that I remember to breathe through it all.

2. But for the Grace of God

Knowing that God's grace and mercy are for everyone, I realize that I had to be willing to receive it. My core belief of not enough was my constant companion for many decades. I had a habit of withholding and withdrawing from everyday life, frequently disguising the low self-esteem as a desire to be hero for the world, especially my family. I prayed in emergency situations, not fully trusting the prayer that I said every day: God grant me the serenity. There were many instances that did take courage and wisdom. God's grace, mercy and favor have been my superhero that always came to the rescue. I am accepting that God's grace is my saving grace in all situations.

3. First Things First

When I examine the process in my mind, I realize that was the issue. First things first—the concept took a while to resonate for me to understand. I just did not get it. My thought was to get everything done at once. Finally, I realized I can't do everything all at once. The importance of first things first is that, in order to get things done, I have to start at the beginning not the middle. I had to figure that out when I began recovery, when I took chemistry, when I bought a house and when I chose to engage in my own personal spiritual development. I had to fill the application out first before I could get to the initial intensive. Being aware of what is in front of me supports me in moving forward. Prioritizing gives me the divine opportunity to make a conscious choice to align with my Creator, through prayer and meditation. Asking for support from my higher self, angels, guides and ancestors, praying, setting an intention and to proceed with grace and ease.

4. Honesty, Open-mindedness and Willingness

These are the three indispensable principles that have made a world of difference in my life. I had to release denial—I didn't even know I was lying; close-mindedness—thinking my way was the only way; and resistance—I just was not ready for the unknown. After taking another moral inventory of where I have been in my life, my environment and what emotional nurturing I received, it became quite obvious why I would have any trouble with these three principles. The clarity moment was admitting I didn't know.

Truth is, once I discovered the root of the truth, I was a volunteer for my own insanity. Waking up to the crazy, eventually I became tired and took a chance at just telling my truth as I saw it. That is when I was open to receive feedback from those who cared enough to tell me what they saw and heard, and I became willing to step out of the box with a neutral eye and see me. Utilizing these principles repetitiously has given me divine makeovers.

5. Nothing Changes if Nothing Changes

If I am to be in the same place, I will never get to another place. I had to shift my vibrational energy in order to make something different occur in my life. I had an expectancy that there must be some inner movement in my mind so that it is pictured in my life. I had to have hope that is bigger than life. I had been in a place that was stagnant and it was a dark abyss where I felt that I was stuck. I became very complacent with not being able to see. One day my eyes opened and I saw a glimpse of light. That is where I had to make another agreement with myself to make a shift that would give me the inspiration and motivation to see and be at another destination in my life. It took one prayer at a time, one step at a time, and one day at a time. I knew that it had to begin within. My thoughts became my reality. A major lesson is that every thought is a prayer.

6. Fear: Face Everything and Recover

Fear has been controlling my life for a long time. I was hiding from my own brilliance, being caught up with what I assumed was in someone else's consciousness concerning me and what and how I was doing and being. Fear told me that withdrawal was the perfect anecdote for my low self-esteem and self-pity. Fear has been my deceptive companion for too many decades. It has been busy conjuring new and innovative means to keep my divinity a huge secret from me. One day I made a choice to look at all that was keeping me away from a bliss-filled life. That meant I had to go through the pain of withdrawal in so many areas in my life. It was time to say yes to the spiritual, mental and emotional surgery, no matter how the physical aspect of me complained continually. I was determined to see things in my world differently. I am facing it all and I am healing. I am acknowledging and accepting where I have been, and I am happy about my future.

7. People, Places and Things

I recall years ago being told by my parents not to associate with certain people because they were involved in illegal activities. I was told that they were trash. I remember becoming that trash. I was told not to hang around bars and clubs and they became the places I frequented most. I was told to stay away from things such as drugs and alcohol. I became addicted. What I did not know or understand is that people, places and things originated in my mind. It was my thoughts that entertained the thought of being disobedient. It was my thoughts that said just maybe if I go with so and so it might be fun. It was my thoughts that said yes to drugs. I made a choice to change my thoughts and my world transformed. My thoughts, actions and words spoken are aligned with spiritual law and principle. My prayer is that God will show me the right people, that I speak the right words and that my actions are pleasing to the Divine. Today I do my best to have my people, places and things align with God's Divine Will for my life.

8. Loving You, Losing Me

In my relationships with others there was a blind spot where I had this insane thought that there was no me without that individual. I have cried many a tear over a love that I believed that I had lost, when in reality, I only attracted what I felt and thought about myself. That moment of awakening came slowly over time;

even after years of recovery, I believed that I was unworthy of being treated like the Divine child of God I know I am today. Learning through the many emotional and mental filters that were in place through my lifetime, I had to be re-educated about who I was and who I belonged to. Having that spiritual awakening and a re-conditioning of my consciousness, I know that today through God's amazing grace and love, I have found the greatest love of all. The essence of my Creator is where I have found me.

9. Denial – Don't Even Know I Am Lying

Living in an illusion of pretense and false manifestations, I encountered many superficial associations with other human beings who, with or without their consent, were convenient bandages for the wounds of the past that I falsely claimed were healed. I assumed, made up, imagined and fabricated that I had this invisible cape that could possibly, if the other party made a choice to pay attention, could be fixed and healed. I had the so-called solution to what ailed anyone except myself. Unknown to me, the covert plan was that I would be in control. This is something that I had no clue about my role in being oblivious to my own melodrama. Thank God for the eyes and ears of divinely appointed folks who have patiently and prayerfully supported my awakening to the experience of who I have been. I am grateful that I can keep the focus on and be present to and for myself.

10. When the Student is Ready, the Teacher Will Appear.

It took years of resistance, dishonesty, judgments of self and others, projections, false accusations, lying, cheating, stealing, low self-esteem, lack of self-respect, very little self-esteem and a twisted definition of self-love to finally take a look in the mirror and see the Dorian Gray that I had been for so long. The pain behind the smile and the hugs became quite evident; I could no longer wear the mask of deception and self-abuse. It was too obvious and more than anything the pain became unbearable. It seemed the only thing that was plausible in my case was total surrender to spiritual laws and principles. My way served no good purpose. I had exhausted all my plans. I was ready, willing and able for Divine intervention. The Holy Spirit stepped in, asked a question, and I said YES. Thank You, God, for knowing!

11. It Works If You Work It

Most things in life take some effort to get a result. I look at my physical body today and I am grateful for the work that I have put in to release fifteen pounds. I am aware that if I had exerted more energy I probably, possibly, may have released thirty pounds. I see where my procrastination and laziness have worked for me also, where I earned a place in the Personal Development Program due to my unwillingness to do the work. That is the bottom line, cut and dry. Anything that is meaningful to me, I will go the extra mile for. I have bent over backwards to be in service to others and, I believed at the time, for God. My spiritual eyes are open now. I have much reverence for my journey. I love me to a greater degree than ever. I honor and trust the God in me. I am no longer afraid to sweat for the glory of God, every moment digging deeper to re-discover who I really am. I am an intuitive, loving woman in whom God is well pleased.

12. Let Go and Let God

One of the hardest things I have found is letting go, simply because I desire to hold on. The thought of letting go means that I have a comfort zone attached to it. It has represented my having to be alone without another, then I would have to go through the pain of withdrawal. It meant that I no longer use my chemical dependency as a crutch to ignore or dismiss the emotional, mental or physical pain or discomfort my humanness was experiencing. It meant releasing old patterns and behaviors that had lost their former pertinence in my life, giving up attempting to control my adult children, forgetting that they received many lessons from me and one main one was to pray for and about any and everything that was on their minds. Letting go and letting God is remembering that every thought is a prayer. I no longer have a need to straddle the fence with God. Having faith and trust that God provides all that I could ever want or need is an act of letting go. As I release all confusion, uncertainty, guilt, shame, doubt, fear, and anxiety, I lovingly, with blessed assurance, affirm with much gratitude and joy my God-reliance, God-dependency and God-confidence. I prayerfully and peacefully surrender to win!

Unfinished Chapter 1

The sweet tune of barbaric order, my concrete environment. Listening to the talking trees engaged with the fluttering songs of the baby red-breasted robins and the brown speckled sparrows as my urban jungle unfolds. The melody of the wind and rain cleansing the polluted air. Who is the stranger here? Still, every day, another blessing. I was born to read. I was born to learn. I was born to teach. Knowledge, understanding, and wisdom—I am more than convinced that these must increase. Always striving to attain thee, it has been my experience that there has been a kaleidoscope of many attributes and principles to master in this learning process. Giving my will and my life over to the God of my understanding means to renovate my inner landscape so that these principles and others along with universal law may occupy and take residence in my soul, my heart and my mind, where God has been all the time.

I was born to find balance while dancing—yes, skipping. I on the cement lines of the urban sidewalk, food squeezing through.

See what I see, dandelions pushing, growing through the city cracks. The prophet Bohannon asked, "Let's start the dance; how low can you go?"

I am a descendant of slaves, ministers, an evangelist, number runners, proprietors of speakeasies, teachers, musicians, drug dealers, builders and royalty. Who am I to sit still and say I am free, when the horrors of the past are present in the now, where the master is the gun and the so-called law of the land has been empowered by money and drugs? Where the American dream is but a dream without faith and action? With God all things are possible.

Who am I with a brain, a soul, a mind, a heart? Who I have become is a woman of God who has walked in fear since I was a child, molested and gang raped. I have learned to cope by being able to hide my true self, forgot my real identity. I am a product of trauma, learned to rob and steal, became a liar to go along to get along, smoked that crack, drank wine and liquor, did my share of hashish, opium, weed, angel dust, and a few tabs of mescaline. I actually held on to the demented and disturbed thought that it was fun until I embraced the pain that insisted that these were copiously needed.

I am the mother of three of the most beautiful, intelligent, and charming individuals in this lifetime. They are my tribe. I love my children and I respect their distinct personalities and individualities. I have shown them my eccentricities, coupled with a bit of drama trauma, abandonment, self-centeredness and mental disengagement. I am sure that I have embarrassed them all with my low self-esteem, twisted thinking and erratic living. These were my choices, some unconscious and unintentional. Even staying clean from mind-altering substances didn't cease the ego distortion of my mind and actions. I had the mental inclination to think I had the ability and capability to accomplish anything I wanted to without the support of others. There was no veracity to this preposterous statement and to add insult, evidence was seriously lacking, not remembering the journey which my ancestors had been through, aches in my bones, the remembrance.

I eventually let my transparency show. Having my child grow and mature in a place called jail, shame and guilt was my dance—why couldn't I set him free? Who am I to want more for my son, an innocent man, yet he was politically drafted; the Pontius Pilate party began. I know my son. I asked the question. They called him a bad boy; my son said, "No Mom, it wasn't my crime." Here is where my heart was broken again when the judge said mistrial. Of course, my perceived thoughts and hopes were that my second born was to be liberated. I had great expectation and anticipation to celebrate his emancipation. They gave him three death sentences; how did they plan on killing him three times? Due to gracious intervention and blessed individuals being able to see his light, that insane sentence shifted from death to life away from the ones he loves. I prayed; I really did need the peace and calm to breathe so that I would hold my tongue not to cuss somebody out and go to jail myself, martyring myself to trade places to accept this injustice as my own. I just wanted him free at any cost. I had nightmares about my young, beautiful prince being in maximum security, confined in such a dark place, a dungeon conjured in my mind from what I had heard, read and saw in movies, documentaries and personal stories.

I have this mother's kind of faith in my son. I believed him then and I know now. The truth will bring emancipation—yes, set him free! My beloved Ibn, a convicted man, chained like a slave—how could this be? I took the blame. I know and understand a powerful message my mother gave me as a gift on plaque. It said, "Always remember that nothing is going to happen today that you and God can't handle together." A couple of years before my son was incarcerated, he survived a murder attempt. He was shot close range in a car. Five bullets penetrated his body. I have one of the bullets that was freed from his body. It was smuggled out of the capital punishment unit of the prison. If that bullet can be released out of his body while he is in prison, I know he will be released too. I felt that was a sign from God. I proudly stand by him now with absolute assurance, as I did then. I pronounce to the world that my Ibn, my hijo, my gift from God, my baby boy, regardless of others' judgment and conviction, is innocent and coming home, for God has plans for him. He has been away for almost a score; time waits for no one. His hair is salt and pepper gray. He is a concerned and loving parent and a stick-his-chest-out doting grandfather.

God did it to Jesus, so why not mine? My son's prison number coincidentally begins with the letters JC, some hope in front of his number. He is a praying man and I know that God is granting him the courage to deal with everything.

It's been a while yet I did not get high, through the years raised in a place of beat the system, my personal hustle didn't get my desired outcome. Gambling was just another drink. God's will, not mine is the only answer. God, you saved him from five bullets, one now in my dresser drawer; because he lived, I praised the Lord yet prayed for others who had a Hail Mary experience. I know I am a woman of God, desiring for the day to bring my son home, to celebrate his grand rising. My baby boy is no longer a child; he is a man of humility with a divine purpose for his soul. His journey the Lord has decreed, countless days of being still in a place called the hole, solitary confinement. Expressing his truth came with a price. His mind is focused and he seeks more clarity; there must be a reason why.

I proclaim it's time for the prison doors to open for my Ibn, my son, my man-child also known as innocent in my deepest consciousness. I have the honor and privilege to be his appointed portal to this place of savage illusions, as his mother, a minister of spiritual God, who knows holiness abides in me, which gives me serenity, courage and strength. I am a mother of one of many innocents enslaved. I was born to experience the sadness and disappointment. I came into this existence to lose my mind and with great ardor and perseverance to locate God. I've gained some wisdom; my daily companions are love, balance, and integrity on the path the Lord has decreed. The Spirit grants me serenity, courage, strength and wisdom to be all that I am.

I am a mother of one of many innocents enslaved. I was born to experience sadness and disappointment. I was placed on this planet to lose my egoistic mind and with great passion and zeal to discover my creator, my Lord, my God is truly omnipresent, for the Divine was with me through the fire and every storm. The Divine's loving Grace is omniscient and omnipotent, giving me the gift of self-compassion, as the prophets continue to sing to my affirmations, my truth, my love, my spirit, my soul, my life. The psalms of Stevie: She hears my cries; she hears the lamentations I have tried so desperately to conceal. Stevie wrote, "I was living just enough, just enough and let's not talk of the rapes and the worldly trauma and the drugs and R&B." And the prophetess Tina sang, "I've been here before, not coming back…no more, no more." Is she sure that the cosmic source won't bring me back?

Still on the journey, I have had so many second chances—they call it Grace—just to be anesthetized and humiliated to perform pirouettes of shame and guilt, resentment and fear with many clever made-up addictive games. At last, I have finally the blessed quandary. There is a source called God living in and through me, my ride-to-die chick, in my own sanctuary. There I find my own innocence and humility. I must go in my closet; there is no doubt I have reached the stars' unconditional self-acceptance and self-love, internally renovated by amazing grace, faith and love. Let me touch me in a gentle way, something I've never felt in my history. Breathing deep within into my soul, so precious I am to me; I did not know that revealing love to the stranger inside, calling my own name to me, I have been the stranger here.

Hello love—the infinite perfection that knows all of me for sure has eased my mind with caresses of abundant comfort, more than enough to honor and be myself. As I embrace the myriad of sensitivities that cloak my mind, heart and soul, I am able to move with divine elegance. I am so blessed, so blessed that the flowers and the butterflies follow every movement of my dance. I now get it at a deeper level. Forgiveness does not keep time. Joyful living comes from within. I only have to understand unequivocal, unconditional acceptance and love. Let me love her like she's never been loved before, simply trust enough to let the sweetness of God to unfold now. Rocking it into me, I see slow dancing with true intimacy and healing, worthy healing choreographed by the Creator of the Universe.

Next rehearsal, the Song of Songs, the intimate relationship with my daughters.

ABOUT THE VISIONARY AUTHOR

ArDenay Garner is a survivor, bestselling author, and personal development trainer committed to promoting compassion and world healing through storytelling and healing conversations. She is the executive producer at Me, Myself & God Tours, Inc., a premier event management company that offers exclusive services to nonfiction authors, and the owner of ArDenay Innerprize LLC, a personal development company.

ArDenay provides book collaborations, coaching, speaking, and consulting services for visionary leaders, entrepreneurs, and organizations whose mission is to eradicate generational trauma and develop human potential. She has hosted numerous events including her signature LOVE Campaigns, award ceremonies, and various seminars and retreats helping over 300 women reclaim their self-confidence.

ArDenay received a Master's in social work at Syracuse University in 2014 and Bachelor of Science in business administration at Columbia College in 2008. ArDenay has received a host of other accolades and recognition throughout her career. Recently ArDenay received the 2022 Sister Mary Vera Award and was voted CNY Remarkable Woman for 2022.

ArDenay is creating a movement of resilient Black women authors who want to unmute their voice, write to heal, and to help others do the same. She currently resides in Upstate New York with her loving husband and children. You can connect with her on Clubhouse in her Resilient Black Women Club having candid conversations about healing, storytelling, entrepreneurship, and creating generational wealth every day at 7:00 a.m. ET.

To learn how you can join the Resilient Black Women Authors movement email ArDenay at ardenay@ardenaygarner.com or visit www.ardenaygarner.com

Facebook: ArDenay Garner
Instagram: ArDenay Garner